Contents

Line references in these Notes are to the Oxford University Press edition of *Shakespeare: Complete Works*, but as references are also given to particular Acts and Scenes, the Notes may be used with any edition of the play.

To the student

A close reading of the play is the student's primary task, but it is well worth seeing a performance if possible. These Notes will help to increase your understanding and appreciation of the play, and to stimulate *your own* thinking about it: *they are in no way intended as a substitute* for a thorough knowledge of the play.

The author and his work

Surprisingly little is known of the life of our greatest dramatist, and the little we can be sure about comes mainly from brief references to him in legal or other formal documents. Though there is no record of Shakespeare's actual birth date, we do know that he was christened William at the market-town of Stratford-on-Avon on 26 April 1564. He was the third child of John Shakespeare – variously described as glover, wool dealer, farmer and butcher – and Mary Arden, whose family were prosperous local landowners. However, until the year 1578, when his business began to decline, John Shakespeare was a notable figure in Stratford, and William was probably educated at the local grammar school – where he would have learned the 'small Latin and less Greek' of which the playwright Ben Jonson (1572-1637) accused him. But John Aubrey (1626-97), in his *Brief Lives* (written in the 17th century but not published until 1813) says that Shakespeare had 'enough education to become a schoolmaster' – and stated categorically that his father was *not* a butcher.

In 1582, at the age of eighteen, Shakespeare married Anne Hathaway, a woman eight years his senior, who bore him two girls and a boy: Susanna in 1583 and the twins Hamnet and Judith in 1585. He is thought to have left Stratford for London in 1585: there is a tradition (which Aubrey does not deny) that Shakespeare had to flee his native town to avoid prosecution for stealing deer in Sir Thomas Lucy's grounds. But, more to the point, it seems that he left with a band of strolling players, the Queen's Players, who visited Stratford in 1585.

Whether he took his wife and children with him to London is not known, but a pamphlet published in 1592 by a lesser playwright Robert Greene mentions Shakespeare as an actor and playwright. Plague caused the theatres to close in 1593; on their reopening in the following year we know that Shakespeare was by then a member of The Lord Chamberlain's Company (known after the accession of James I as The King's Men). It is probable that he stayed with this company throughout the remainder of his career, writing plays and acting in them in various theatres. His connection with the company must have brought him considerable financial reward, and Shakespeare seems to have been a good businessman as well, for when he retired to Stratford in 1611, aged forty-seven, he was already a fairly wealthy man and a shareholder in two theatres, the Globe and the Blackfriars. He purchased New Place, one of the largest houses in Stratford – where he entertained Ben Jonson and the poet Michael Drayton (1563–1631), and – by the astute purchase of tithes and arable land – he became, in the tradition of his maternal forefathers, a prosperous landowner. He died in Stratford-on-Avon on 23 April 1616, survived by his wife and two daughters.

As an actor Shakespeare does not seem to have been particularly successful; but even in his own day his fame as a dramatist and his personal popularity were great. In 1598 Francis Meres (1565–1647), the writer of critical assessments of playwrights, described Shakespeare as 'the most excellent in both kinds' [i.e. in comedy and tragedy], and even Ben Jonson, whose dramatic work was in a very different vein, remarks of Shakespeare in *Discoveries* (1640), 'I lov'd the man and do honour his memory (on this side idolatry) as much as any.' And John Milton (1608–74) wrote in his poem 'L'Allegro' (1632) the often-quoted lines: 'Or sweetest Shakespeare fancy's child/Warble his native woodnotes wild.'

Shakespeare probably began his work as a dramatist by collaborating with others and patching up old plays for his company to revive. His first completely original play is believed to be *Love's Labour's Lost* (?1590), though the date of each play presents a problem: the dates are not given in the First Folio (the first collected edition of his plays, 1623). His first narrative poems, composed during the Plague when the theatres were closed, were *Venus and Adonis* (1593) and *The Rape of Lucrece* (1594). His 154 *Sonnets* were published in 1609 – without Shakespeare's permission, it is said. The first 126 of these intensely personal poems are addressed to a young man, the poet's friend and patron; the remainder to a 'dark lady'. The identity of neither of these two inspirers of the sonnets has been established – nor has it been decided how far the series is autobiographical.

Most of the plays were written for performance in the public playhouses, and were conveniently classified in the First Folio in three groups: comedies, histories and tragedies. But these divisions are too arbitrary – the 'comedies' can contain tragedy, the 'tragedies' moments of mirth, and the histories have aspects of both tragedy and comedy.

When, however, the plays are considered chronologically they fall naturally into four periods. From about **1590–93** Shakespeare was **learning his trade** while patching up existing plays and beginning to write his own: to this period belong *Love's Labour's Lost*, *The Comedy of Errors*, *Two Gentlemen of Verona*, the three Parts of *Henry VI*, *Romeo and Juliet* and *Richard III*.

From about **1594–1600** was the period of Shakespeare's **greatest development**, when he wrote such plays as *Titus Andronicus*, *A Midsummer Night's Dream*, *The Merchant of Venice*, *The Taming of the Shrew*, the two *Parts* of *Henry IV*, *The Merry Wives of Windsor*, *As You Like It* and *Twelfth Night*.

Despite what we have said above, the period **1602–08** can be described as that of **the tragedies**, which include *Hamlet*, *Othello*, *King Lear*, *Macbeth* and *Antony and Cleopatra*.

Shakespeare's **final period (1610–13)** includes three romances: *The Tempest*, *Cymbeline* and *The Winter's Tale* and one historical play, *Henry VIII*.

As for the original productions of these plays, Shakespeare cared little about the dress of his characters – irrespective of place or period, the actors wore the English fashions of his time. And, whatever might be a play's geographical setting, his clowns and lower-class characters were true London cockneys or British country bumpkins – such as would appeal to the gallery in English playhouses.

Since that time, there have been many fashions in 'dressing' the plays: there have been attempts at contemporaneous setting and clothes – in more recent times some of the plays have been produced against stark backgrounds and in modern dress. But today there is a movement towards vaguely 'historical' dress, and (after decades of sonorous, sometimes pompous and often unintelligible speaking of the lines) to a simpler, more naturalistic delivery, such as Shakespeare's original players probably used.

But, notwithstanding the many and various innovations over the years, Shakespeare's genius, his lyrical lines and wonderful choice of words, his warmth and his understanding of the human predicament, continue to bring entertainment and enlightenment to people all over the world.

Norman T. Carrington MA

Brodie's Notes on William Shakespeare's

King Henry IV
Part I

Pan Books London and Sydney

First published by James Brodie Ltd,
This edition published 1976 by Pan Books Ltd,
Cavaye Place, London SW10 9PG
    3 4 5 6 7 8 9
ISBN 0 330 50005 8
Filmset in 'Monophoto' Baskerville 10 on 12pt and
printed in Great Britain by
Richard Clay (The Chaucer Press) Ltd, Bungay, Suffolk

The play

Plot

Henry IV, Part I continues the story of *Richard II*. Three of the Percy family, Thomas, Earl of Worcester, his brother Henry, Earl of Northumberland, and the latter's son, nicknamed Hotspur, are stung by the ill-treatment afforded them by King Henry IV, who has made use of their services to depose Richard II and gain the throne for himself, and then has coolly cast them off. They therefore plan a rebellion against the King. The main plot of the play deals with the hatching of the conspiracy, leading to the battle of Shrewsbury, in which Hotspur and Worcester, allied with a Scottish Earl, Douglas, are defeated by the King, Hotspur himself being slain by the Prince of Wales.

At the beginning of the play the Prince spends most of his time with frequenters of taverns, and there are some lively scenes of low-life, the life and soul of which is a fat knight, Sir John Falstaff. These scenes make the sub-plot (or comic plot). The serious fight of the serious plot is balanced by a comic fight in the comic plot. Falstaff and others of the tavern set arrange a high-way robbery of some rich travellers, but the Prince and one of his friends contrive in turn to rob them of their booty, for the sake of 'the incomprehensible lies that this same fat rogue will tell' about the odds of the encounter. Everything turns out as expected.

When the rebellion breaks out the Prince has to turn his mind to more important things, and even Falstaff goes on active service and appears at the battle of Shrewsbury.

As the play continues the story of *Richard II*, so does it look forward to *Henry IV, Part II*. Although the King has won this battle, there are still other conspirators under arms, and the play ends with the King's plans to conquer them, which are put into effect in *Henry IV, Part II*.

The historical period of the action of *Henry IV, Part I* was nearly twelve months, between the battle of Holmedon, 14 September 1402, and the battle of Shrewsbury, 21 July 1403.

Source of Plot and its Treatment

The historical events are taken from Holinshed's *Chronicles of England, Scotland and Ireland*. The following are Shakespeare's chief alterations, all for a dramatic purpose.

1 Hotspur and the Prince are made of an age. Actually Hotspur was older than the King. In 1403, when the battle of Shrewsbury was fought, the King was thirty-seven, Hotspur thirty-nine, the Prince fifteen and Prince John fourteen. In the play the King speaks of crushing 'our old limbs in ungentle steel' (V. i. 13), and Hotspur and the Prince are represented as young men. This throws into relief the contrast between them, which is the chief character-interest of the serious plot throughout. One would expect differences of outlook between an old man and a young man; by making these two of the same age the differences of character are made to stand out more clearly.

2 The interview between the King and Hotspur (I. iii) is made to take place at the palace, where the King was when he announced his intentions concerning Hotspur (I. i), instead of at Windsor. This concentrates similar scenes at the same place.

3 The reconciliation between the Prince and his father comes much earlier in the play than in Holinshed. In the play this scene is made the turning point in the transfer of our sympathies from the rebels' to the King's side, and it is largely as a result of his promise to his father in this scene that the Prince turns to worthier things.

4 The events connected with the battle of Shrewsbury which go to exalt the Prince (his challenge to Hotspur and those mentioned on pp.76–7) are of Shakespeare's invention. Here he wants everything to point to the Prince's glorification and triumph. Similarly Shakespeare increases our regard for the King and our joy that the 'right' side has won by making the King more generous to a defeated foe than was actually the case. No mention is made of the historical fact that Hotspur's dead body was placed between two millstones, and afterwards beheaded and quartered.

5 New characters are introduced.

a) Falstaff and the 'comic' characters, for the sake of contrast with the serious plot (see below).

b) Lady Percy and Lady Mortimer, to give variety in a play of men characters.

Of course, there is nothing in Holinshed of Shakespeare's characterization. Here we see not historical figures of the past but men and women whom we should know in a thousand.

Structure

The King is the first speaker, and he makes known the situation at the start of the play (see p.29).

In Act I the serious conspiracy, which provides the action of the historical plot, is planned, and also the comic conspiracy against Falstaff, which provides the action of the sub-plot. The central figure of the historical plot is Hotspur, of the comic plot Falstaff.

Contrast is a fundamental principle of Shakespearean drama. Notice particularly the following contrasts.

1 Between historical plot and comic plot. Comic and serious scenes jostle one another through this play (as they do in life), making the comic show up more comic against the serious and the serious more serious against the comic. The student should notice the disposition of the scenes of the main and the sub-plot.

2 Between characters.

a) The two groups of characters – the court group and the tavern group.

b) Certain individual characters, e.g. the Prince and Hotspur, the Prince and Falstaff. (Also foils are introduced, e.g. Douglas is brave but not so brave as Hotspur, Prince John is brave but not so brave as the Prince of Wales, and thus the bravery of Hotspur and the Prince of Wales respectively is thrown into relief.)

c) Methods of dealing with characters, e.g. Hotspur's character takes us by storm all at once, whereas that of the Prince is gradually revealed. At the beginning of the play we sympathize with Hotspur, but our sympathy for Hotspur decreases until we have less sympathy for his side than we have for the Prince's – the turning point is the scene where Hotspur is so quarrelsome and the rebels plan to cut the land up; on the other hand, our sympathy for the Prince increases – the turning point being the following scene, where he makes his promise to his father.

Plot and sub-plot must not only serve as a contrast to each other, they must be well bound together, otherwise the play will be 'broken-backed' and fall apart into two separate plays. In *Henry IV, Part I* the main and the sub-plot are dovetailed into one another. The Prince is the chief connecting link between the two plots.

The climax of the comic plot is the unmasking of Falstaff's lies about the fight against his unknown assailants. Note that the climax is not the actual fight. 'The virtue of this jest will be,' says Poins, 'the incomprehensible lies that this same fat rogue will tell us when we meet at supper.' He never once hints that the point of the joke will be the joys of laying Falstaff flat, but the 'reproof' of Falstaff's lies when he comes back to the tavern. The climax of the comic plot comes much earlier than the climax of the serious plot, as if Shakespeare was much more interested in it. Shakespeare's comic plots usually develop faster than his serious ones.

The student would do well to make a list of the characters which appear (1) only in the main plot, (2) only in the sub-plot, (3) in both plots.

In every play there is a clash of personalities or of wills. Notice the threefold clash in this play, (1) in the King's country, (2) in the King's home, (3) in the King's mind (the sense of guilt, particularly apparent in III. ii).

Theme

The theme of *Henry IV, Part I* seems to be the quest of honour.

Hotspur shows off in his pursuit of honour, shouting out from the house-tops how

> it were an easy leap,
> To pluck bright honour from the pale-faced moon,
> Or dive into the bottom of the deep,
> Where fathom-line could never touch the ground,
> And pluck up drowned honour by the locks.

The Prince talks about it little; he pursues it quietly, calmly and resolutely: honour to him consists in *doing* an honourable deed, quite apart from who knows about it or 'the bubble reputation' (see p.77). To Falstaff honour is 'a word', 'a mere scutcheon', and his whole life tallies with his conception. He will 'none of it'. 'Give me life,' he says, and the winning of honour is of no account beside the saving of his own skin.

Setting

The local colour of all Shakespeare's plays is that of Elizabethan England, whether the story is one of England, Italy or Denmark, and in whatever age. Nowadays we should demand strict accuracy in scenery, costume and topical references, but then, for playwright and audience alike, the life and spirit of a play mattered more than strict accuracy in local colour. 'It is the spirit which giveth life.' People saw in the drama a reflection of their own life and experience; its appeal was in no wise analytical or educational, but human and curiously personal.

Further, in those days people were untravelled and un-educated, and anachronisms would not strike a false note in an age more familiar with the stories than with their settings.

And it must be remembered that there was no scenery and no period costume. Incongruities which become apparent beside 'realistic' scenery would not be noticed then, and references to a character's dress must be to something that he was actually wearing on the stage.

Henry IV, Part I takes place historically in the early fifteenth century, but we are never very far from the London that Shakespeare knew. The dress of the landlord of the Boar's Head, described humorously by the Prince to Francis (II. iv), is contemporary, certainly not 'period', costume, and in the same scene there are references to psalm-singing weavers, morality plays ('a dagger of lath') and another early Elizabethan play ('King Cambyses' vein'), and the 'watch'. These can be paralleled in all parts of the play. But more important than specific allusions like these is the Elizabethan atmosphere throughout. The early morning inn-yard scene (II. i) is thoroughly Elizabethan, in fact all the tavern scenes have a strongly Elizabethan flavour.

Characters *King Henry IV*

Anointed majesty.

At first the King has little to recommend him. Insincerity peeps through his strained, self-conscious speeches, and before long is proved by facts (see p.29). Hotspur and his father and uncle have good grounds for offence if the King has treated them as they say – used their support to serve his ends in gaining the throne and then when he had the power cast them aside – though in this connection it must not be forgotten that they had helped Bolingbroke in the hope of getting something for themselves. The source of their resentment now is not that Henry IV is an impostor but that he has failed to give them what they expected for their aid. So long as it suited his purpose Bolingbroke led them on with promises; when he no longer needed them he let them know it. He has gained the throne as much by diplomacy as force of arms, and himself admits as much to his son (III. ii). There is thus much justice in Hotspur's taunts, 'this ingrate and canker'd Bolingbroke,' 'this king of smiles,' 'this fawning greyhound.' At the beginning of the play our sympathies are wholeheartedly with the rebels. The King has treated them shabbily. Ambition like Hotspur's that is ready to run risks wins admiration, while cunning that is ready to take advantage of others earns contempt.

The King shows that he is superstitious, in spite of his shrewdness. Mortimer, he says, must have turned traitor and made it up with Glendower, whom he went to fight; he could never have fought him, for

> He durst as well have met the devil alone
> As Owen Glendower for an enemy.

This is manifestly inconsistent, too. If the King knew that Mortimer could not possibly defeat such a 'great magician', why did he countenance his expedition?

Realization of his 'mistreadings' gives the King some pangs of conscience (III. ii. 4–11), causes him to keep to himself and makes him suspicious of others. Others may have such designs on his throne as he had on that of Richard II and be working them out secretly all unknown to him, just as he did when he plotted against Richard. Even his own son comes under suspicion. He cannot stand the stiff formality of the court, he wants to laugh and be natural, both of which the deliberate and cautious Henry IV can never do. Henry IV feels all the more lonely because he is not in the confidence of his son, and as a result accuses him of being

> like enough, through vassal fear,
> Base inclination and the start of spleen,
> To fight against me under Percy's pay.

The comparison between the Prince and Richard II, both consorting with the common people, is only too apparent. By the 'never-dying honour' of his exploits Hotspur becomes a popular idol, while by familiarity with 'rude society' his own son brings contempt upon himself. History is likely to repeat itself within one generation. So it seems to the King, who, previous to their interview, at any rate, has not been able to discern the true nature of his son.

> For all the world
> As thou art to this hour was Richard then
> When I from France set foot at Ravenspurgh,
> And even as I was then is Percy now.

Opposition puts him on his mettle and brings out the best in the King. With his hands 'full of business', in supreme command he makes quick, definite decisions, which give him a great advantage over the rebels with their divided counsels. Further, however he obtained the throne, now that he has it he considers the welfare of his *whole people* – 'We love our people well.' His enemies consider only themselves and seriously entertain a mad plan to carve up the land according to their whims and fancies, without any consideration that the country is the home of people. At least the King stands for ordered, regular government, 'limit and true rule', 'anointed majesty'. He tries to avoid bloodshed with 'gracious offers', which we somehow feel this time are sincere, although the rebels, perhaps consistently, feel that they cannot place any reliance in the promises of a man who has made promises before and snapped them at will.

> The king is kind; and well we know the king
> Knows at what time to promise, when to pay.

When the King finds himself to have been in the wrong in his suspicions of his son's loyalty, he freely acknowledges it. He takes the Prince to his heart and by so doing wins a warmer place in our hearts.

At the end – after a rather self-righteous rebuke to Worcester and Vernon (see note on 'Thus . . . rebuke,' p.80) his strength lies in trying to restore order without rancour or hatred, meting out justice tempered with mercy.

The Prince of Wales
Redeeming time when men think least I will.

The Prince inherits one side of his father's character, his diplomacy. 'Mad-cap' he may be, but that there is method in his madness appears from his speech closing Act I, Sc. ii. No one would deny that he thoroughly enjoys tavern life, but from this speech the design in his life is clear.

> So, when this loose behaviour I throw off
> And pay the debt I never promised,
> By how much better than my word I am,
> By so much shall I falsify men's hopes;
> And like bright metal on a sullen ground,
> My reformation, glittering o'er my fault,

Shall show more goodly and attract more eyes
Than that which hath no foil to set it off.
I'll so offend, to make offence a skill;
Redeeming time when men think least I will.

Meanwhile he is free to enjoy himself as he likes, and he is only too glad to escape from the restraint and formality of his father's court to the riotous mirth of the Eastcheap tavern. He prefers to be clapped on the back and called 'Hal' rather than be saluted ceremoniously as 'Your Royal Highness'. Amongst Falstaff and the rest he can give full play to his love of adventure, his sense of humour and his good-humour. From the first, however, he is not unmindful of the high position which he will one day be called upon to fill, and moulds even the full and free enjoyment of the tavern to suit his ultimate purpose. He seems to have himself well in hand. He holds his true character in reserve, then, when good qualities seem to be added later in life, they will be all the more precious to the people for having been unexpected. As John Bunyan says, 'The bitter goes before the sweet, and, forasmuch as it doth, it makes the sweet the sweeter.' The change in the Prince's character is not so sudden as we may think. Rather is it that certain latent qualities show themselves. When he did become King it would surely help him that, noble as he was, he had a knowledge of ostlers and drawers, for he would be king of them as well as of earls and prelates, and, indeed, many more of them than of earls and prelates.

The Prince, it is urged, never puts his hand to anything really base. At the time of his triumph there is nothing in his past which detracts from it, nothing which is more than the pranks of a high-spirited youth. This is no doubt the dramatic reason for Shakespeare's adoption of a plan which leaves him out of the actual robbery of the Travellers. After the robbery it is the Prince who decides that 'the money shall be paid back again with advantage'. But would he have done so had the Sheriff not been on the track of it? And how far does he use his public position for private ends? Had he not been Prince of Wales there is little doubt that the Sheriff would not have taken his word that Falstaff was not in the house, but would have brushed him aside and carried out his search. He tells the Sheriff a barefaced lie. Whatever the Sheriff suspects, he cannot go against the word of the Prince of Wales. And when the Prince promises to make Falstaff answerable to the Sheriff in person by 'to-morrow dinner-time', he knows from the news he has just received from court that by to-morrow dinner-time the land will be astir and both he and the Sheriff will have more important things to do than bother with Falstaff. We excuse the Prince's lie because without it Falstaff will be imprisoned. We do not know the Sheriff or the Travellers; Falstaff has a warm corner in all our hearts; we should not like to see the rascal locked up.

From Act III onwards the Prince seems to be a different man. He stands with square shoulders before his father when he is summoned to answer for the 'barren pleasures' and 'rude society' of his life. As he holds up his head in the pride of his purpose, we feel that 'self-reverence, self-knowledge, self-control' of which Tennyson speaks. (Study this interview carefully. See also pp.56–7.) Still, his heart may be right, but so far he has no achievements to his credit. When the time comes we see that what his heart purposes his hand is ready to carry out, that he 'never promiseth but he means to pay'. We feel that he is worthy to be set in charge of men. (This is helped by contrast with Falstaff.) If there is a time for foolery there is a time for seriousness, and when Falstaff hands him a bottle of sack instead of a pistol on the battle-field, for the first time his fun meets with no response.

The Prince is able to smile at 'the Hotspur of the north; he that kills me some six or seven dozen of Scots at a breakfast, washes his hands, and says to his wife "Fie upon this quiet life! I want work." ' The Prince's underlying common sense and sense of proportion are part of his strength. While Hotspur blusters, the Prince, calm, courageous and resolute, finally achieves his purpose. The Prince shows a nobler strain than Hotspur, for whereas Hotspur chafes whenever the Prince is praised, the Prince is ever generous and chivalrous in his estimate of a brave foe, and modestly under-values himself by the side of him. 'Our antagonist is our helper,' says Burke: at all events, through his antagonist the Prince becomes the man now he had intended to be only when he became king. Had the rebellion not broken out there is little question but the Prince would still have been in the tavern. Instead, he is challenged to his best and highest, becoming finer in spirit, more generous in service, more wishful to live splendidly. Hotspur's courage and dash, of which everyone knows, is matched by the Prince's courage and coolness, of which no one knows. He loves honour every bit as much as Hotspur but pursues it in a different way (see pp.4–5). In contrast with Hotspur he *talks* little of honour. Honour for him consists in the *doing* of an honourable deed, not in being in the limelight for it. The conflict is hard, but on that very account the triumph is more glorious. For a detailed study of the Prince's triumph in the battle see pp.71 and 76–7. Hotspur is made to 'render every glory up', and if Falstaff wants to get the medals for it he is welcome to them. 'True bravery,' says Emerson, 'is often best shown by performing without witness what one might be capable of doing before the world.' In the hour of his triumph notice the Prince's modesty (V. v. 19). Reviewing the battle he casually speaks before his father and the chief lords of 'The noble Percy slain' – not a word of the identity of the slayer. If anyone had drawn attention to it, he would no doubt have said that it was all in the day's work.

Surely when this man takes the helm, the ship of state will be in good hands.

Hotspur
Gunpowder Percy.

The Prince's character is revealed gradually: Hotspur takes us by storm all at once (see pp.3–4). Hotspur is first pitted against the King, and the two stand in marked contrast, the impatient, slap-dash nature against the coldly rational, the imaginative, impulsive mind against the administrative and calculating. Nothing more than his description of the King's representative on the battlefield after the battle of Holmedon, or of Mortimer's fight with Glendower on Severn's banks, need be cited to show his vivid imagination. His disjointed speech in the first of these two scenes, particularly after the King has left him with a burning sense of injustice, admirably expresses the volcanic stuff in his nature. At the end of Act I he stands out with a pride in a purpose new begun, as the Prince does in Act III Scene ii, but it is a pride more flashing and ostentatious, perhaps more self-conceited.

Hotspur needs directing. He is energetic, but too impatient to be up and doing, a man unfitted to sit down and consider and plan his efforts. He lives all the time in a ferment, like a great and strong wind, an earthquake and a fire, without the still, small voice. Look at the way he stamps and shouts in Act I Scene iii and refuses to let anyone else get a word in. He goes at everything like 'a bull at a gate'. One imagines his declamatory speeches to be accompanied by gesticulations right and left. Enthusiastic himself, Hotspur is just the man to rouse the spirit of the troops and sustain their morale for battle. But a rebellion needs careful organization. This is where Worcester excels. Imagine the effect of cold-blooded Worcester on a troop of soldiers! His part is the planning behind the scenes, Hotspur's the actual leadership. 'Malevolent' Worcester, more far-seeing, knows this, and easily makes a tool of Hotspur for his purposes, fans his resentment and makes a lasting hatred out of what might have been a momentary 'flare-up' (see p.35). He is afraid, however, that Hotspur's enthusiasm may carry him into indiscretions. Note his warning before the conspirators separate, 'No further go in this than I by letters shall direct your course.' That the warning was needed appears from Act II Scene iii where Hotspur has committed a fatal error in writing to an unsure lord, who will now lay the rebels' plans before the King. He has learnt his lesson, and now, impulsive as he is, goes right to the other extreme, and will not tell even his wife where he is going next.

Hotspur's treatment of his wife seems rough superficially but is not really unkind. There is more banter in it than anything else. If she wanted, Lady Percy was quite capable of meeting him on his own ground, as when Hotspur in amused contempt mimics Mortimer and his wife (see p.53) She evidently thought him a bit of a 'bounder'. Until recently Hotspur has kept his wife informed of developments (see note on 'my brother . . .

title', p.45), so that evidently there was a feeling of mutual trust between them. Even if we did not know this we should gather it from her remonstrance with him now for not trusting her; she does not take it as a matter of course, so that it would appear that Hotspur was not in the habit of keeping things from her.

Forgetfulness and impatience accompany such a nature

> What do you call the place? –
> A plague upon it, it is in Gloucestershire;
> 'Twas where the madcap duke his uncle kept,
> His uncle York; where I first bow'd my knee
> Unto this king of smiles, this Bolingbroke, –
> 'Sblood! –
> When you and he came back from Ravenspurgh.

He suddenly remembers that he should have brought a map, when he gets to the Bangor conference, and the same expression gives vent to his impatience.

> A plague upon it!
> I have forgot the map.

At Bangor, Hotspur's fiery truculence and outspokenness nearly wreck the conference. He goes out *looking* for trouble and never stops to think. He squabbles just when it is a time for them all to pull together. Now is no time for bitterness or misunderstandings. He is quick to show his feelings, either of joy or anger, and when small things irritate him he does not remember the greater issues at stake and keep his self-control. He does everything on the spur of the moment. He makes things more difficult than they are already for other people, besides himself. Vanity makes a fool of Glendower. A wiser man than Hotspur would have thought it and said nothing. Hotspur must tell him so, and that at a moment when Glendower's co-operation is a dire necessity. He *will* have his own way in the division of the land – like a spoilt child who thinks that someone else has a larger piece of cake – and then, when he has got it, adds insult to injury by declaring that it does not matter after all. On his own admission he is one of those who will 'cavil

on the ninth part of a hair', or, in Hamlet's words, 'find quarrel
in a straw'. Worcester is quite just in his rebuke to Hotspur
while Glendower is away (III. i. 179–80), a passage which
should be learnt as an estimate of Hotspur's character. Hotspur
would control men, yet he could not control himself. Contrast
the Prince, who was the leader of his own soul before he was a
leader of men.

Judging from how things are shaping when Blunt enters,
Hotspur again would have got his own way as to the time of the
attack at the battle of Shrewsbury, not by convincing his confederates of the wisdom of his plan, but by over-riding all
opposition. Vernon has already given way before Hotspur's
personality (although he has taken up his argument again and
begged reconsideration), when the launching of the attack is
suspended by the decision to discuss the King's terms of peace.

Hotspur keeps in good heart, outwardly at any rate, against
Worcester's defeatism (see pp.63–4). He is ready to fight the
world in arms alone. Worcester has no illusions about the peril
of their position, but Hotspur hopes against hope to the end.

A sense of strain clings about Hotspur. He has not learnt the
value of relaxation. See how the anxiety of the rebellion (and
perhaps more the necessity of keeping silent about it) preys on
his nerves and wears him down.

> Tell me, sweet lord, what is't that takes from thee
> Thy stomach, pleasure and thy golden sleep?
> Why dost thou bend thine eyes upon the earth,
> And start so often when thou sitt'st alone?
> Why has thou lost the fresh blood in thy cheeks?
>
> .   .   .   .   .   .
>
> Thy spirit within thee hath been so at war
> And thus hath so bestirr'd thee in thy sleep,
> That beads of sweat have stood upon thy brow,
> Like bubbles in a late-disturbed stream;
> And in thy face strange motions have appear'd,
> Such as we see when men restrain their breath
> On some great sudden hest.

Can one imagine the Prince affected like this? The Prince knew the value of relaxation – all great leaders do. Remember how Brutus, in *Julius Cæsar*, asked his boy attendant to play his lute on the eve of battle. Brutus lost the battle, it may be argued, but then, so did Hotspur.

A rapid, active, impulsive nature of this kind is usually full of contradictions. Chivalrous, Hotspur yet has not the finest flower of chivalry to pay due tribute to an opponent. Himself wanting 'to wear without corrival' all the dignities of honour, when Vernon speaks the praises of his 'corrival' he stops him testily with

> No more, no more: worse than the sun in March,
> This praise doth nourish agues.

He can, however, recognize bravery in Douglas, who is an ally. Of an intensely imaginative nature, showing itself in language burning with poetry, Hotspur affects that he would

> rather hear a brazen canstick turn'd,
> Or a dry wheel grate on the axle-tree;
> And that would set my teeth nothing on edge,
> Nothing so much as mincing poetry.

No doubt he wants to be considered a real 'he-man'. Having much in common with Glendower's Celtic temperament, he yet ridicules Glendower's claims to be 'not in the roll of common men'. The man who speaks of 'swift Severn's flood',

> Who then, affrighted with their bloody looks,
> Ran fearfully among the trembling reeds,
> And hid his crisp head in the hollow bank
> Bloodstained with these valiant combatants.

applies cold, remorseless, matter-of-fact logic to Glendower's claims.

Yet, when all is said and done, there is much likable and something great about Hotspur. Tactless he may be, nevertheless we cannot but admire a man who speaks his mind without fear or favour. This type of man is surely to be preferred to a scheming Bolingbroke or Worcester, who would have been 'tactful' with potential allies. He is not without a sense of humour, as we have seen from his delightful parody of Mortimer and his wife: then there is his inimitable reply to Glendower's

> I can call spirits from the vasty deep.
> But will they come when you do call for them?

It is his sense of humour which gives him a sense of ordinary human values, and helps to keep his feet on mother earth and save him from soaring into a world of his own above the clouds. It makes him see the maudlin sentimentality of Mortimer's behaviour and the childish vanity of Glendower's pretensions. Humour, logic and ridicule make Glendower look small when he wants to look big.

Hotspur's one regret in death is not the loss of life but loss of his 'proud titles'. The differences between his quest of honour and that of the Prince have already been dealt with (pp.3–4). Hotspur has, as he says, lost youth and titles, and is food for worms, but there is nothing dishonourable in his defeat and death, and

> this earth that bears thee dead
> Bears not alive so stout a gentleman.

Honour lasts longer than life; it is eternal, nothing can touch it. Referring to his end at the hands of the Prince, Sir John Masefield, the Poet Laureate, says, 'the soul like clay triumphs over the soul like flame'. Passing over the antithesis, the comparison with flame certainly fits the soul of Hotspur. He trembles at white heat all the time.

Kipling has a line, 'Who are neither children nor gods, but men in a world of men.' Hotspur is now a child, now a god, but never a man in a world of men.

Falstaff

I am bewitched with the rogue's company. If the rascal have not given me medicines to make me love him, I'll be hanged (Falstaff of Poins).

The world is not made just for passionate young men eager for honour. The stout bodies of self-indulgent old sinners find a place in it also. Shakespeare sees the world as it is. In the world there is room for Hotspur and room for Falstaff.

We ought not to like this 'grey iniquity', but we all do. He is not the sort of person whom we should care to have as a friend, but he endears himself to our hearts by his irrepressible good-humour, his sense of fun and sociability. By hook or by crook he means to get the most out of life.

He is devoid of any sense of honour. Honour to him is 'a word' (see p.5). His only object in life is to eat, drink and be merry. A rogue and a thief, he is equally capable of a highway robbery or the more subtle form of robbery seen in his un-scrupulous misappropriation of the King's money. His leader-ship of his soldiers is unpardonable, and to get out of the battle and 'finish early' he sends a hundred and fifty men to their deaths without turning a hair (if he is to be believed). Even after this gross betrayal and wanton disregard of human life, he has the face to follow 'for reward'. Patriotic motives, such as those of the Prince, would be quite incomprehensible to Falstaff.

Yet he makes us laugh so much that we forgive him and just give ourselves up to his fun. Our attitude to him is the same as that of the Prince – 'Were't not for laughing, I should pity him,' and 'I could have better spared a better man' (for the dramatic reason for this, see pp.19–20). He enjoys life if anybody ever did. His breezy presence keeps us in high spirits. His gaiety and good-humour never fail. He never takes offence, never loses his temper, is never angry, takes everything in good part, including barbs at his own expense, most of them about his figure. His mind is as agile as his body is cumbersome. He never has to put a strain upon himself to give a pointed rejoinder. It comes like lightning. He enjoys getting himself out of scrapes by his nimble wit. Pun follows pun. Opprobrious epithets leap to his lips. He is as clever at mimicry as at repartee, as, for instance, when taking off the Prince answering for his behaviour before the King.

Part of the fascination Falstaff exercises on us is due to the sense of surprise that clings about him. We never know what he is going to do or say next.

Half the humour arises from his build, very often emphasized by contrast, for instance, in association with the slim young figure of the Prince, or followed by his company of bare-bones (who, however, do not appear on the stage).

'A goodly portly man, . . . and a corpulent; . . . his age some fifty, or, . . . inclining to three score,' Falstaff still keeps young in spirit because he finds life well worth living and helps others to find it the same.

The following considerations come to mind in any estimate of Falstaff's character.

1 Is he a liar? The question is 'Does he expect to be believed?' For example, is he seriously trying to deceive when he makes 'eleven buckram men grown out of two'; when he quaffs off his sack, puts down his empty cup and a minute or two later says, 'Give me a cup of sack: I am a rogue, if I drunk to-day'; or when he declares that he has killed Hotspur? To the editor it is an untenable position to say that he does. He 'exaggerates' for fun. He delights in make-believe. If his lies land him in a fix, all the better, he can then enjoy inventing plenty more to get him out of it and carry him on a step further. Similar comic make-believe is seen in such speeches as the following.

> They hate us youth . . . What, ye knaves! young men must live.
> A plague of sighing and grief! it blows a man up like a bladder.
> Company, villanous company, hath been the spoil of me.

No one would maintain these as 'lies'.

In this connection contrast the many lies of Falstaff and the one great lie of Worcester. There are five liars in the play, Falstaff, Worcester, the Prince, the King and Blunt, six including Vernon for his tacit agreement with Worcester's lie to the King. Yet all the lies these people tell have a different effect upon us. The Prince lies to the Sheriff, about which there is something to be said on both sides (see pp.9–10), and agrees to support Falstaff in his assertion that he killed Hotspur, 'if a lie may do thee grace'. That is, the Prince agrees to support the lie of another person, just as Vernon does; but how differently do we judge them, admiring the one as much as we despise the other, as the reason for these lies and the motive behind them differ! Blunt lies to Douglas, saying that he is the King, in a patriotic effort to assist the King's tactics and protect the King's person. Loyalty means more to him than life itself. We judge him not by his lie but by his selfless devotion to duty. It all depends on the motive of the lie. Falstaff's lies are humorous, intended to deceive no one; they are sheer comic exaggeration for the fun of it. The others hope to be believed and are judged according as their motive is base or noble.

2 Is he a coward? After robbing the travellers, he remains fighting against the Prince and Poins in disguise. From what he knows of Falstaff, Bardolph, Peto and Gadshill, Poins anticipated that Falstaff would hold out longer than some.

Well, for two of them, I know them to be as true-bred cowards as ever turned back; and for the third, if he fight longer than he sees reason, I'll forswear arms.

(Which two he means he does not say, but probably it is Bardolph and Peto. Falstaff is certainly 'the third'.)
    Falstaff's cowardice in the battle is irrefutable.

3 Has he any self-respect? At first sight he has none, but he has sufficient to be ashamed to march through Coventry with his 'hundred and fifty tattered prodigals'.

4 Has he regard for the Prince? Is his love of the Prince's company genuine, or just for the advantages to him of such a friendship? It certainly keeps him out of the hands of the Sheriff in the play, and, as Gadshill says,

There are other Trojans . . . the which for sport sake are content to do the profession some grace; *that would, if matters should be looked into, for their own credit sake, make all whole.*

Falstaff's jealousy of Poins is undoubted. A desire for the Prince's notice and attention, and a corresponding jealousy of anyone else who comes between him and the Prince, might be said to go with a genuine or an interested affection.
    Dramatically Falstaff is a contrast to the Prince and the serious plot (a contrast in a different way from Hotspur).

Shakespeare had to make him attractive, but not a hero, or he would usurp the place of the Prince.

Style

Professor Dowden has an excellent summary of the development of Shakespeare's style.

In the earliest plays the language is sometimes as it were a dress put upon the thought—a dress ornamented with superfluous care; the idea is at times hardly sufficient to fill out the language in which it is put; in the middle plays (*Julius Cæsar* serves as an example) there seems a perfect balance and equality between the thought and its expression. In the latest plays this balance is disturbed by the preponderance or excess of the ideas over the means of giving them utterance. The sentences are close-packed; there are 'rapid and abrupt turnings of thought, so quick that language can hardly follow fast enough; impatient activity of intellect and fancy, which, having once disclosed an idea, cannot wait to work it orderly out'; 'the language is sometimes alive with imagery.'

Henry IV, Part I is one of the middle plays.

There is not a great deal of beautiful poetry in *Henry IV, Part I*, though there is much of a noble and stately kind. The beautiful poetry is spoken chiefly by Hotspur, many of whose speeches are worth committing to memory. In spite of the fact that he would 'rather hear a brazen canstick turn'd, or a dry wheel grate on the axle-tree' than 'mincing poetry', it is Hotspur who gives us the beauty of such a passage as

> Three times they breathed and three times did they drink,
> Upon agreement, of swift Severn's flood;
> Who then, affrighted with their bloody looks,
> Ran fearfully among the trembling reeds,
> And hid his crisp head in the hollow bank
> Bloodstained with these valiant combatants.

or the bravado of

> By heaven, methinks it were an easy leap,
> To pluck bright honour from the pale-faced moon,

> Or dive into the bottom of the deep,
> Where fathom-line could never touch the ground,
> And pluck up drowned honour by the locks.

The richness and vividness of the imagery of the poetry is to be noted. The similes and metaphors have that sense of surprise and yet of fitness which characterizes the imagery of a genius. Hotspur's imagery, as, for example, the two personifications quoted above, often shows a deeply and strikingly imaginative nature. As Worcester says, 'He apprehends a world of figures.' But he is not the only one. Notice the quick succession of similes in Vernon's description of the Prince setting out for battle (IV. i. 97–110), or the more developed comparisons in the Prince's last speech in Act I Scene ii.

In a good play the style naturally reflects the character of the person speaking, and even the same man in two different moods may speak in two different ways. Look at Hotspur's abrupt and disjointed speech when he is in a temper, as, for instance, after the King's departure in Act I Scene iii, and contrast this with the rather stiff, dignified speech of the King, representing the established order, or even with Hotspur's own speech to the King earlier in the scene, before he was roused. Similarly contrast Hotspur's impetuous speech (and colloquial diction) when he is irritated by Glendower (III. i) with the regular verse of his speech to Blunt (IV. iii) which shows a calmer mood.

There are fashions in literature as in everything else. A pun has been defined as 'the lowest form of wit', but in Elizabethan times punning was extremely popular. Here, at all events, it provides much amusement in and around taverns. The double meaning is generally quite obvious, but in cases of difficulty owing to changes in the language an explanation is given in the notes.

Use of Prose
The normal form of Shakespeare's plays is blank verse. When prose is used it is for a definite purpose.

Prose is invariably used for

1 Comic characters (e.g. Falstaff) and

2 Characters of lower social position (e.g. Poins, Gadshill, Peto, Bardolph and the Hostess).

This was a literary convention at a time when literature was aristocratic and the chief characters in plays (as in life) were kings and nobles. Scenes in which the lower orders of society figure are a contrast; these people live on a lower plane of feeling than that of the main characters, and thereby emphasize the height of the feeling of the main characters, and the contrast in the medium of expression – prose instead of verse – is in perfect keeping.

3 Letters, formal addresses, etc. (e.g. the letter to Hotspur, II. iii).

There is a considerable amount of prose in *Henry IV, Part I*, owing to the large number of humorous scenes. The changes from verse to prose and prose to verse in the various scenes should be carefully studied and reasons for them sought. Act II Scene i and Act IV Scene ii, humorous scenes, are entirely in prose. Notice how in Act I Scene ii prose is the medium until the Prince is alone at the end, and then he speaks in verse: he is away from his low-born companions and, in addition, his thoughts in this speech strike a higher note. It is curious that the Prince speaks in verse also at the end of Act II Scene ii. In Act II Scene iv the Prince speaks in verse to the Sheriff but prose to all the rest. At the end of Act III Scene iii he turns to verse when his enthusiasm for his heroic mission bursts out, in fact even Falstaff speaks in verse here for once. In Act V Scenes i, iii and iv the Prince speaks in prose to Falstaff, otherwise invariably in verse.

Shakespeare shows complete mastery of style and diction. They are equally suited to the dignified scenes of the main plot and the comic scenes of the sub-plot. Further, there are no ups and downs, there is one high level of excellence.

The Elizabethan theatre

At the time of Shakespeare there were probably not more than five public theatres in the land, all in London, and they were built according to the design of the inn-yards of the period, which had been found marvellously convenient places for the presentation of plays.

The theatre was circular or octagonal in shape. The main part of the auditorium was the large round pit, open to the sky, in which the poorer people *stood* (the 'groundlings'). Encircling this, round the walls, were three balconies, covered on top but not in front (like the 'stands' on a football ground), and con-

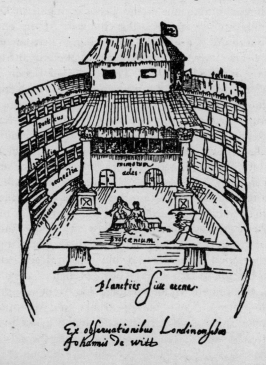

taining seats. Admission to the pit was one Elizabethan penny, while proportionately higher charges were made for the balconies. When it was wet the performance was postponed until the next day.

The stage was large, jutting far into the pit, and was without scenery and any but the most meagre properties. Hence it made no difference that people stood at the side of the stage as well as in front. The scenery was created in the imagination of the audience by the words of the characters in the play: it was made part of the play, so as not to obtrude and destroy the illusion of reality.

The play went straight on without intervals. It should be remembered that on Shakespeare's stage there were no separate scenes *as such*. In the early part of the present century his plays were presented with elaborate, often spectacular, scenery, and sometimes the audience would become impatient at the constant delays while it was being changed. At the present time there is a return to a simple stage setting, in keeping with that of Shakespeare's day, as, for instance, at the Royal Shakespeare Theatre, Stratford-on-Avon. There is good reason to believe that when they were first produced the plays took considerably less time than they do today. The Prologue to *Romeo and Juliet*, for instance, refers to 'the two hours' traffic of our stage'.

The end of a scene was frequently marked by rhyming lines, as in Act I, scenes 2 and 3. Just as the scenery had to be *put into* the words of the play, so had entrances and exits to be arranged as *part of* the play. In a modern play an actor can get into position before the rise of the curtain, but on the open stage it would seem artificial if he walked on and then started his first speech, or finished the scene and then walked off. Such endings as II.1, clear the stage and at the same time fit in perfectly naturally with the action of the play. It follows that dead bodies always had to be carried off the stage in the action of the play.

It was not unknown for the stage floor to be equipped with a trap-door for the sudden appearance and disappearance of ghosts and spirits, and some theatres had a flying apparatus by which such could descend on the stage with the aid of ropes on runners.

At the back of the stage was a recess 'within', and this was curtained and could be shut off when desired. The recess would, no doubt, serve for Poins when he 'stands close', as directed by the Prince, II.2.3, and there is the definite stage direction 'Within' for Poins in Act II.4. Later in that scene Falstaff would go there when he hides 'behind the arras'.

Above the recess was a balcony, which served for castle walls, an upper room, and such scenes. This, too, could be curtained off. Judging from the way opportunities are made for balcony scenes in Elizabethan plays (though not, actually, in *Henry IV, Part I*) people were very fond of them, particularly when there was an escape from the balcony – an upper room, for example – to the main stage – representing the ground below.

People who wanted to be in the public eye were able to hire stools actually on the stage itself. An extra payment entitled them to have their pipes lit by a page, thus showing to all and sundry that they were in a position to be attended. Such a privilege would be valued by country gentlemen who wanted it to be known that they had come up to town. It was a source of continual annoyance to playwrights that actors 'gagged' in order to please these aristocratic playgoers.

Women were not allowed to act by law. Consequently women's parts had to be taken by boys with unbroken voices. Considering the limited emotional range of a boy's voice, imagine a boy's rendering of Lady Macbeth or Cleopatra or Desdemona – or even of Hermia and Titania. The ban on actresses accounts for the few women's parts in plays of the period, though some were always introduced for the sake of variety. In King Henry IV, Part I, there are only three, though history plays naturally offered a predominantly male cast. It also accounts for the large number of plays where a woman disguises herself as a page boy. It made it much easier for the producer; further, the audience was intrigued by a situation in which a character was pretending to be what he really was! In *The Merchant of Venice* every one of the women disguises herself as a man.

Plays were not acted in period costume, though frequently *some* attempt was made to suggest a period, and the result must often have been a bizarre compromise. Thus all Shakespeare's plays can be said to have been first acted in 'modern dress'. Although there was no scenery, managers spared no expense on the most lavish of costumes.

On days when the theatre was open a flag was flown from the turret, and when the play was about to begin a trumpet was sounded. The turret of the Globe Theatre housed a big alarum bell, a favourite theatrical effect. This would be the bell that rang out the alarums in the battle in Act V.

The text of Shakespeare's plays

Few readers of Shakespeare realize the difficulties scholars have had to overcome in order to establish accurate texts of the plays. The First Folio (see pp.iv–v) contained thirty-six plays. Other collected editions or Folios were published in the seventeenth century, the Third and Fourth Folios containing seven additional plays, none of which, with the exception of *Pericles*, is now thought to be by Shakespeare. Sixteen of the plays had already been published separately as Quartos before 1623, and in the case of some plays, for example *Hamlet*, more than one Quarto edition exists. Some of these Quartos are almost word for word the same as the texts in the First Folio and were possibly set up from Shakespeare's own manuscript or at least from accurate theatre copies; but others are shortened, inferior versions, possibly 'pirated' editions published by some unauthorized person who had access to theatre copies or parts of them, or who had taken down the plays in shorthand while they were being performed. It is thought that the texts of the First Folio were set up from the good Quartos and from good theatre copies. But these texts must all be compared, printers' errors and other interference traced, before a reliable text can be arrived at. The first editor to attempt the problem of the text was Nicholas Rowe (1674–1718), who also divided most of the plays into acts and scenes, supplied indications of entrances and exits, and lists of dramatis personæ, which are absent from many of the texts in the Quarto and Folio editions. *Henry IV, Part I* is one of the few plays divided into acts and scenes in the Folio, indeed, it is just as in our modern editions except that Scenes ii and iii of Act v are combined. Act and scene divisions are convenient for reference (like the division of the books of the Bible into chapters and verses) but have no important use in Shakespearean study. They were fitted for the stage of Rowe's time, but were unnecessary upon Shakespeare's stage with the barest of scenery.

Notes

Act I Scene i

Henry IV has deposed Richard II, and has since been engaged in 'mopping up' operations.

At the opening of this scene the King welcomes peace at home in order that he may embark on a crusade, but almost before the words are out of his mouth he calls for the decisions of the previous night's council to be made public to his attendant lords. There it was decreed that, owing to Mortimer's defeat and capture by the Welsh under Glendower, the crusade was to be abandoned for the time being. Further news is that Hotspur, having beaten the Scots, has refused to give up his prisoners. News of both battles at once gives an impression of general disorder on all sides.

At the outset the King's insincerity is apparent, for he would have attended the council and at the very moment when he was giving thanks for the internal peace which would make it safe for him to undertake a crusade he evidently knew that it was out of the question. He had also heard of Hotspur's defiance, and anticipates trouble from that quarter (ll.92–95). The projected crusade no doubt provided a good excuse to keep men under arms.

The King who gives the title to the play is the first speaker. In Shakespeare's earlier plays this is usually so. Later Shakespeare introduced minor characters who spoke about and 'led up' to the main character before his appearance. This method has the advantage of creating suspense, and when the main character appears he appears in response to a longing of the audience to see him. He thus makes a greater impression. From a practical point of view it also means that the first speeches of the main character are not disturbed by the entrance of latecomers: by the time he speaks the audience has 'settled down'.

Notice the first adjectives applied to some of the chief characters, which stamp our first impression of them – ll.38, 40, 52, 53, 62, 97. Later on, ask yourselves how far first impressions prove lasting.

care a stronger word than now – 'anxiety'.

Find we let us find.

pant have a breathing space. The idea is that even while peace is panting for breath she tells of new tumults to come. The metaphor is from a hunted animal stopping to get its breath back, thus 'short-winded'.

stronds strands.

trenching cutting the earth into trenches ('channels').

eyes Synecdoche.

of one nature, of one substance i.e. countrymen. The war was a civil war.

close encounter, getting at *close* quarters.

mutual well-beseeming united as they should be.

his i.e. war's.

master owner.

impressed enlisted.

levy levy *and* lead.

bootless in vain.

Therefore we meet not that is not our purpose of meeting.

cousin used loosely of any relationship in Elizabethan England. So to-day a man calls a boy 'son', without any suggestion of the actual relationship.

dear expedience important lightning expedition.

hot in question being eagerly discussed.

limits of the charge estimates of the cost.

athwart at cross purposes, interfering with our intention.

post messenger. Messengers used to be stationed with horses at intervals (their 'posts') along a road, for the quick despatch of letters by a series of fresh horses, as in a relay race.

Against . . . Glendower Historically the battle was fought on 22 June, 1402 (at Pilleth, near Brynglas, Powys).

corpse corpses.

uneven hard to bear.

Holy-rood day Holy-cross day, 14 September, which, according to tradition, commemorates the restoration to Jerusalem of a fragment of the cross of Christ by the East Roman Emperor Heraclius. Chosroes, King of Persia, had carried it off as plunder when he sacked Jerusalem in 614, but in 627 Heraclius defeated Chosroes, and the sacred relic was recovered.

approved tested, well-proven.

Holmedon Humbleton, about a mile west of Wooler, Northumberland.

sad serious.

by judging from.

shape of likelihood as it was likely to turn out.

contention 'close', 'broil'.

any either.

industrious consistently and earnestly loyal.

new lighted just alighted.

he hath brought us So that the King was aware of impending trouble with Hotspur, as well as Glendower, when he made his first speech. See p.29.

smooth and welcome A contrast with Westmoreland's 'uneven and unwelcome', l.50.

Balk'd piled up.

Earl . . . Menteith Really 'Earls': four separate earls are meant.

a prince Notice how casually Westmoreland makes this remark, which leads to something dramatically so important. The natural transition in the conversation to the contrast between the Prince and Hotspur adds greatly to the impression of reality.

minion favourite.

Plantagenet Surname of the royal family at the time. This dynasty held the throne from 1154 until 1485.

let him from keep him from, prevent him from entering.

coz Contraction of 'cousin'. See note p.30.

none but Mordake Earl of Fife The reason for this exception was that the Earl of Fife was a member of the royal family.

aspects respects.

prime preen. With 'bristle up the crest', a metaphor from a bird.

for this cause See p.29.

on Wednesday next. Windsor Such little circumstantial details give the truth of fact to a play.

Act I Scene ii

Here we are introduced to the comic plot. The ne'er-do-wells of the play plot to waylay some travellers on the highroad. The Prince and Poins secretly counter-plot to leave the actual robbery to Falstaff and three others, and then, disguised, to rob *them.* The purpose of their jest, Poins says, is to hear the 'incomprehensible lies' Falstaff will tell of the encounter.

At the very end we get a glimpse of a latent noble ambition in the Prince, in spite of his wild pranks and love of the tavern. Coupled with this is a hint of scheming diplomacy, not surprising in a son of King Henry IV.

As we turn from the nobles at the court to the comic characters, and also characters of low social position, whose usual haunt is the tavern (though not here), there is a change from verse to prose. But notice how, when the Prince is left alone and the theme of his speech has a smack of nobility, he speaks in verse.

demand . . . know ask for what you really want, i.e. you ask what time of day it is, whereas all you are concerned with is the time of *night*, to which Falstaff agrees.

come near me are quite right, i.e. I stand corrected, or, as our slang expression has it, 'That's one on me.'

the seven stars A cluster of small stars called the Pleiades.

Phœbus Greek sun god.

'that wandering knight so fair' Probably a quotation from a ballad popular in Shakespeare's time. Though allusions in Shakespeare's plays may be difficulties for us, we may be sure that they were not for his audience.

prithee Contraction of 'pray thee'.

grace Falstaff uses the word in three senses, (1) as a term of address to a noble, (2) meaning 'devoutness', (3) meaning 'grace before meat'.

egg and butter boiled egg and bread and butter.

roundly plainly.

Diana Roman moon goddess.

minions See note p.31.

countenance Used in the sense that the moon 'countenances' it.

holds well as we say, 'holds good'.

'Lay by' Pretended to be spoken to the travellers or persons being robbed.

'Bring in' Pretended to be spoken to the inn-keeper, telling him to bring in more sack.

ladder i.e. of the gallows.

ridge cross-beam.

Hybla The name of several small towns in Sicily.

old lad of the castle The original Falstaff was called Sir John Oldcastle, the name of a knight who suffered martyrdom in 1417, but Shakespeare altered the name by royal command, as a result of protests of a descendant of Sir John Oldcastle.

buff leather. The point of the Prince's remark is that the sheriff's officers usually wore buff jerkins.

robe of durance A pun on a hard-wearing robe that *endures* a long time and a prison dress.

quips smart retorts.

quiddities hair-splittings, quibbles.

here apparent. heir apparent The student will notice many puns of this nature. See p.21.

resolution . . . law determined men thus put off, as they are, by the deterrent of out-of-date laws.

brave fine.

jumps agrees.

court Punning on a court of justice and the palace court. 'Suits' continues the punning, meaning firstly favours asked of a monarch, and secondly suits of clothes.

'Sblood A contraction of 'God's blood' – an ingenious way of getting round a law which forbade the profane use of the name of God on the stage.

gib tom.

lugged led, pulled, i.e. from place to place in a travelling show.

hare Proverbially melancholy.

Moor-ditch An open drain in Moor-fields, London, noted for its bad smells.

comparative given to making comparisons or 'similes'.

vanity emptiness, waste of time.

commodity consignment.

wisdom . . . regards it See *Proverbs*, I. 20–24.

an if.

'Zounds Contraction of 'God's hounds'. See note on ' 'Sblood' above.

one i.e. one of the party.

baffle me put me to shame.

set a match made an appointment.

Remorse Poins had not heard Falstaff's regrets for his past life. Evidently they were typical of him.

agrees Strictly speaking, should be 'agree', but in Elizabethan English a word is frequently attracted to the nearest word and not the whole sense.

cozening cheating, lit. pretending to be a man's 'cousin' (relative – see note p.30) in order to get something out of him, a form of confidence trick as common in Elizabethan times as to-day. cf. 'coz', note p.31.

Gadshill It is rather confusing to have the same name for a character and a place in the play. Shakespeare never bothered much over trifles like this.

pilgrims going to Canterbury They would be going to the shrine of Thomas à Becket, the most popular medieval pilgrimage in England. Chaucer's *Canterbury Tales* were written less than twenty years previous to the time when the events of *Henry IV, Part I* took place.

vizards masks.

lies lodges.

in Eastcheap i.e. at the Boar's-Head tavern.

I will stuff . . . crowns i.e. after the robbery.

Yedward Edward (Falstaff is speaking to Poins).

one See note above.

want countenance i.e. need the 'countenance' of people of influence and substance. For 'countenance', cf. note p.32.

All-hallown summer All Hallowmas (All Saints' Day) is 1 November. The meaning of the metaphor (and of 'latter spring') is that though old in years (in the autumn of life) Falstaff is young in spirit (in the spring or summer of life).

like likely.

habits dress.

appointment part of our outfit.

cases suits.

for the nonce for the occasion. A corruption of 'for then once'.

inmask cover as with a mask, disguise.

noted well-known (no sense of 'famous').

doubt fear.

the third i.e. Falstaff.

virtue point.

incomprehensible boundless.

wards guards, i.e. warding off blows in fencing.

reproof denial, proving false.

I know . . . See pp.22 and 32. Notice the three comparisons which the Prince draws in his speech.

unyoked uncurbed, unrestrained. Metaphor from the yoke of a beast of burden.

humour mood, fancy, inclination.

contagious harmful.

accidents incidents.

the debt I never promised i.e. people thought that he would never reform, his early life gave no promise of it.

sullen ground dull background.

o'er i.e. the 'reformation' is compared to the 'bright metal' and the 'fault' to the 'sullen ground'.

skill sensible thing to do.

time i.e. my past life.

Act I Scene iii

The King takes Hotspur to task for making the surrender of his prisoners conditional upon the King's ransom of Mortimer, his brother-in-law. He leaves Hotspur abruptly with 'Send us your prisoners, or you will hear of it.' In his anger Hotspur falls an easy prey to Worcester's schemes for a rebellion. Hotspur finds out for the first time that Mortimer was proclaimed heir to the throne by Richard II. One of the chief grievances of the rebels is that Henry IV has made use of their help to get the throne and then cast them off.

Hotspur's character sweeps us off our feet, as it does all who come into contact with him. Bluff, impetuous and over-bearing, he soon gets 'worked up', yet has a vigour and dash which holds us.

blood temper.

temperate mild.

tread upon strain.

myself i.e. considered according to my position.

condition natural disposition.

young down the fluffy feathers of young birds.

holp helped.

portly important.

moody threatening.

servant brow brow of a servant. With 'frontier' forms a military metaphor.

use assistance.

Holmedon See note p.31.

deliver'd reported.

envy malice.

misprision misunderstanding.

pouncet perfume.

Took it in snuff i.e. I took it in snuff, an idiom meaning 'I was annoyed at it.'

holiday affected.

with owing to.

popinjay parrot.

grief pain.

God save the mark An expression of impatience. Literally it meant 'God prevent the birth-mark', a prayer of expectant mothers for their children.

thing i.e. to cure. The normal order would be 'thing on earth for an inward bruise.'

parmaceti spermaceti.

tall brave, much in the same sense as we use the word 'stout'.

come current Metaphor from coinage, i.e. be accepted as genuine.

so if.

Who ... fight See I. i. 38–42.

Earl of March Mortimer (though historically Mortimer did not hold this title).

indent with fears sign an agreement, i.e. come to terms with people whom we fear.

starve die (not necessarily through lack of food).

one penny cost the expenditure of one penny. 'One' is emphatic.

fall off fail in his service, i.e. he *did* fight Glendower and not make a pact with him.

one. all Notice the antithesis.

mouthed gaping.

confound spend.

changing hardiment exchanging blows.

breathed stopped for a 'breather'. Cf. 'pant', p.30.

Severn Notice the personification here and elsewhere in Hotspur's speech. It shows an imaginative mind. So does his picturesque description of the lord who came up on the battle-field after the battle of Holmedon.

crisp i.e. rippled.

colour i.e. so as to hide it and make it look innocent.

belie lie with regard to.

He durst . . . enemy Why then did the King let him go? cf. this inconsistency in the King's words with that in Sc. i. See also p.7.

kind manner.

license permit.

An if 'An' means 'if' (see note p.33), so that one of these words is redundant.

after straight go after him straightway.

ease my heart 'get it off my chest.'

Albeit although, lit. although it be that.

make a hazard of risk.

Re-enter WORCESTER. He has evidently been hovering around waiting for the King's departure, so that he could seize his opportunity.

'Zounds See note p.33.

want lack.

on his part on his side, for him.

ingrate ungrateful.

canker'd rotten, as the bud of a flower is eaten out by a canker-worm.

Bolingbroke Henry IV, who was born at Bolingbroke, in Linconshire. It was customary for members of the royal house to take the name of their birth-place.

forsooth in truth.

eye of death death-like look.

in from.

Irish expedition Richard's second Irish expedition, undertaken in May 1399.

intercepted prevented from carrying out his purpose.

soft A common exclamation of Shakespeare's time.

that set . . . man See also Hotspur's speeches IV. iii. 54–98, and
  Worcester's speech V. i. 32–71.

murderous subornation perjury causing murder.

second secondary.

ladder See note p.32.

gage pledge, engage.

both i.e. nobility and power.

canker dog-rose. Not used with the same meaning as 'canker'd',
  I. 137.

shook shaken.

disdain'd disdainful.

answer pay.

cousin See note p.30.

unclasp The metaphor brings to mind a book locked by means of a
  clasp, and therefore containing something very secret.

conceiving understanding. Your discontent will make you quick to
  grasp it.

As full of peril . . . spear Notice how the cunning Worcester tries
  to get Hotspur's support. No enterprise could be so sure of Hotspur's
  support as one with a spice of adventure and peril.

fall in Continuing Worcester's image of the 'current'.

or sink either he must sink.

So honour cross it provided that honour crosses its path.

corrival rival, competitor.

half-faced half-hearted.

form We should say 'substance'.

attend listen to.

cry you mercy ask your pardon.

I'll keep them all. The very mention of his Scots prisoners sets
  Hotspur off again. It is a long time before anyone else can get a
  word in.

gall and pinch Metaphor from the chafing of a horse by his harness.

sword-and-buckler Contemptuous, like 'swashbuckler'.

Nettled stung by nettles.

pismires ants.

what . . . place A slight but very real touch, especially from the
  headstrong Hotspur.

kept lived.

'Sblood See note p.33.

Ravenspurgh A town on the Yorkshire coast, where Henry IV, then
the banished Duke of Bolingbroke, landed for his invasion of England.
It now lies under the sea to the north of Spurn Head. At one time it
must have been a place of importance (though not necessarily of
population) as it sent two members to Parliament.

candy deal of courtesy The normal order would be 'deal of candy
(candied) courtesy'.

cozeners See note on 'cozening', p.34.

mean for powers means for (raising) soldiers.

estimation Explained by the next clause.

occasion opportunity.

game . . . slip Metaphor from letting loose greyhounds after their
prey.

still always – the usual meaning in Elizabethan English.

head army. Punning on 'heads' earlier in the line.

even correctly.

home back.

no further . . . course Worcester knows Hotspur's rash nature. He
has good reason to wonder where it will lead him. Later on it is
Hotspur's breaking the news of the plot to someone not sure that
leads to its discovery.

suddenly shortly.

powers armies. See note above.

I trust Contrast this with Hotspur's 'Upon my life, it will do well',
and 'In faith it is exceedlingly well aim'd'. Northumberland is
half-hearted from the start.

O, let the hours . . . sport Just like Hotspur; he wants to dash off
straightaway. Assuredly Worcester is the man to plan a conspiracy,
as Hotspur is the leader to inspire enthusiasm in his soldiers. In a
rebellion both have a part to play.

fields i.e. battle-fields.

Revision questions on Act I

1 What is the evidence for the assertion that the King's first
speech is sheer hypocrisy from beginning to end?

2 What are the first adjectives applied in the play (by West-moreland) to Mortimer, Glendower, Hotspur, Archibald, Worcester?

3 Where is the first contrast made between Prince Harry and Harry Percy? Who makes it, and to whose advantage?

4 Show how Shakespeare quickly puts the audience in possession of the chief threads of the plot in the opening scenes of the play.

5 Contrast the tone of the beginning and the ending of Scene i.

6 Why is the Prince's last speech in Scene ii in verse?

7 Describe how Worcester makes a willing tool of Hotspur.

8 What is your opinion of (a) Hotspur, (b) the Prince, at the end of the Act?

Act II Scene i

After a realistic Elizabethan early morning inn-yard scene, the Chamberlain comes in and shows that he is in league with the robbers of Act I Scene ii, as he corroborates information already given to Gadshill of wealthy travellers on the Road. (Conditions like these, where innkeepers are in league with robbers, may be compared with those in Charles Reade's novel *The Cloister and the Hearth*.)

Little circumstantial details make this early morning inn-yard scene as real as could be – 'Cut' chafed by his saddle; the uncertainty of the carriers as to the time; their alertness (no doubt due to experience) against pilferers; their impressions of their night's lodging, especially as the house is under new management. Things are not what they were: since the death of Robin, the old ostler, hastened by an increase in the price of oats, the peas and beans are dank and it is 'the most villanous house in all London road for fleas'. (cf. note on 'on Wednesday next. Windsor', p.31.)

an See note p.33.

Charles' wain the Great Bear. 'Wain' = wagon. Notice the method of telling the time in an age when clocks and watches were uncommon.

beat i.e. so as to make it pliable.

Cut The name of a horse.

point pommel.

out of all cess beyond all measure.

next surest, *lit.* nearest.

bots horse disease caused by parasitic worms in the animal's intestine.

joyed was joyful.

since the price of oats rose This is thought to allude to the corn famine of 1596, and, if so, helps to fix the date of the play. No doubt there are many topical references in Shakespeare's plays which gave a 'spice' to contemporary audiences but are quite lost on modern audiences.

tench Supposed to be infested with parasitic vermin.

christen Christian.

cock cock-crow.

razes bundles of roots.

faith reliability, trustworthiness.

Nay . . . faith He fears that he will not see his lantern again. For 'soft', see note p.37.

Sirrah carrier . . . London Notice how casually Gadshill tries to get information so important to the robbers.

will wish to go.

great charge merchandise of great value. For 'charge', see p.30.

holds current holds good. Cf. note p.36.

franklin small land-owner. Originally a franklin was a landowner of free but not noble birth.

wild weald.

marks A mark was worth 67p. Mention of the actual number of marks—three hundred—is one of those circumstantial details which strengthen the impression of reality.

eggs and butter See note p.32.

presently immediately (the literal meaning).

Saint Nicholas 'old Nick'. Thus 'Saint Nicholas' clerks' are thieves.

John Falstaff.

starveling starved person.

Trojans Slang for 'thieves'. When Gadshill refers to the 'other Trojans', he is, of course, thinking of the Prince.

foot-land rakers robbers who go about the land on foot 'raking in' what they can get.

long-staff sixpenny strikers robbers who strike a man down with a long staff for a mere sixpence.

mustachio with moustaches.

tranquility those who live at ease, and are therefore men of substance.

oneyers accountants.

hold in stand their ground.

make her their boots In the double sense of walking on her and using her for their good.

foul way a muddy road.

liquored greased. The pun is obvious.

receipt recipe.

fern-seed Supposed to make invisible those who carried it.

beholding beholden.

purchase Euphemism for 'plunder'.

'homo' Lat. for 'man'. Apparently Gadshill means that all are men, irrespective of whether they are true or false, implying that there is not much to choose between them.

Act II Scene ii

This is the scene of the robbery, and everything turns out as foreseen by Poins in Act I Scene ii.

The robbers meet. Even with a robbery on hand, there is time for fun, and Poins plays a practical joke on Falstaff by hiding his horse. They disguise themselves, and the Prince and Poins slip off according to plan. Falstaff and the three left are successful in robbing the Travellers; but immediately the tables are turned as they are attacked and robbed by the Prince and Poins, just as Falstaff is declaiming against their cowardice in slipping out of danger.

It is a scene with plenty of action and plenty of fun. Falstaff cannot resist getting amusement even out of the attack on the Travellers, interposing his very blows with lively banter, very comical to us who know him.

frets wears himself away.

gummed i.e. stiffened; 'starched' is the modern equivalent.

close hidden.

squier foot-rule.

for in spite of.

starve See note p.36.

colt fool.

uncolted As he is without his horse.

ta'en captured (because unable to escape on horse-back).

peach impeach, turn evidence against them and implicate them in the crime.

afoot Punning on the jest's being afoot and his being so.

setter the one who has 'set a match'. See note p.33.

Case ye encase yourselves, i.e. in your masks.

vizards See note p.34.

make i.e. make prosperous, set up for life. Falstaff adds a tag altering the sense.

happy man be his dole may he be happy. 'Dole' = lot.

the boy . . . hill A practical necessity, to avoid bringing horses on the stage.

caterpillars The sense is that they eat up the goodness of the land.

bacon Standing for luxury.

gorbellied big-bellied.

chuffs boors, churls.

bacons Suggested by any 'gammons of bacon' these Travellers were carrying (?).

You are grandjurors, are ye? Evidently in reply to a threat of law action by the Travellers, or perhaps to a statement of their position to show that an attack on such people was a serious matter and would be taken up vigorously by the Sheriff's officers.

jure make jurors of.

argument a topic.

An the prince . . . stirring Notice the irony here, in view of what follows immediately.

Got with much ease Why is this speech in verse?

lean Probably implying that even the earth is lean by the side of Falstaff.

Act II Scene iii

Hotspur is reading a letter from a luke-warm lord, whom he has approached to join the rebellion. The letter is non-committal, and Hotspur fears that now the writer will take his news to the King, who will thus be in a better position to forestall the rebels. As Hotspur reads the letter he gives way to many jerky expressions of impatience and contempt at the lord's shallow cowardice. Incidentally, we learn that the conspirators are due to meet 'by the ninth of the next month'.

Lady Percy enters and tries to find out what it is that has been worrying her husband for the last fortnight. He will not tell her, however, and refuses to be taken seriously, repelling her earnest pleas with rough banter. She has come at a bad time, just when Hotspur has found out that he has given valuable information to an unreliable person. Thus, even if he would have satisfied his wife's pleading previously, he is proof against it now. The situation is serious, the rebels' intentions in the hands of an enemy, maybe: perhaps in his haste to be getting on with something, Hotspur had not adhered to Worcester's advice.

> No further go in this
> Than I by letters shall direct your course (I. iii. 292–3).

The realization that the King may already know of the plans of the rebels determines Hotspur to set forward within two hours.

The introduction of a scene with different characters between Scenes ii and iv gives an impression of the passing of time, so that by the beginning of Scene iv it seems that the Prince and Poins have had ample time to get back to the tavern. This is one of the chief dramatic functions of a sub-plot running parallel to a main plot. You will find several other examples in the play (e.g. I, ii between the King's announcing that he has sent for Hotspur and Hotspur's appearance before him).

there i.e. at some meeting-place with the rebels.

unsorted ill-suited.

counterpoise of so great an opposition so great an opposition counter-balanced against you on the opposite side.

expectation promise.

sincerity of fear and cold heart A pointed way of expressing

Hotspur's sarcasm. He means that he will go *really* in 'fear and cold heart' but *with an appearance of* sincere loyalty to the King.

go to buffets i.e. one half of myself against the other, as we say, 'kick myself'.

stomach appetite.

thick-eyed Because the eyes are dull (not bright and sparkling, as we imagine Hotspur's to be) when one is 'musing'.

Speak terms of manage give commands. 'Manage' = management.

retires retreats. A noun.

palisadoes palisades.

basilisks heavy artillery.

culverin cannon with a long barrel.

currents changing fortunes.

hest command.

What ho! A call for the Servant.

back get on his back.

straight straightway. cf. 'after straight', note p.37.

Esperance Hope (Fr.) Motto and war-cry of the Percies.

weasel . . . spleen The weasel was proverbially irritable and morose.

my brother . . . title Evidently Hotspur had trusted his wife with the secret of Mortimer's claim to the throne, which he had found out himself only in Act I, Sc. iii.

title i.e. claim to the throne.

line support.

paraquito parrot.

An if See note p.37.

mammets dolls.

tilt with lips The metaphor implies that there is *real* tilting to be done.

crowns Another metaphor from currency (see note on 'come current', p.36, and 'holds current', p.41), suggested by the double meaning of 'crown' ('head' and the coin).

pass them current i.e. they must be given and taken, like current coin of the realm.

God's me A contraction of 'God is for me'.

What say'st . . . me? She evidently restrains him from going.

whereabout for what purpose.

of force perforce.

Act II Scene iv

This scene is the one most full of fun in the play. As a prelude, the Prince tells how he has been below-stairs learning Eastcheap slang. Then, with Poins, he plays a practical joke on Francis. But it is with the entrance of Falstaff, accompanied by the rest of the thieves, all looking as if they have been in a fierce fight, that the real fun begins. Everything happens as Poins had predicted. In Falstaff's account the two attackers become a hundred, and it turns out that it is Falstaff who has persuaded his companions to 'beslubber' themselves with blood and hack their swords to give credence to their tale. Even the thieves cannot agree as to what really did happen. Falstaff himself gets hopelessly involved as lie succeeds lie, and, finally, the Prince's 'plain tale' shatters his pack of lies completely. But the fun is not so much in the 'incomprehensible lies' of Falstaff as the way he gets himself out of the tight corners that they get him into. He is never at a loss: he can always find some 'trick', 'device' or 'starting-hole'. How could he see his adversaries were dressed in Kendal green when it was so dark that he could not see his hand? – He will give no man a reason on compulsion, 'if reasons were as plentiful as blackberries, I would give no man a reason upon compulsion, I'. He recognized the true Prince, but

was it for me to kill the heir-apparent? should I turn upon the true prince? why, thou knowest I am as valiant as Hercules: but beware instinct; the lion will not touch the true prince.

At the height of the fun we are made to realize that the Falstaffian comedy is not a play on its own but an integral part of a play founded on historical events. The comic and the serious plots are brought into relation when the hilarity is interrupted by the Hostess, who announces that a nobleman from the court is at the door. He has come with a message for the Prince to go back to court on account of the rebellion.

Falstaff tries to make the Prince's flesh creep by exaggerating the seriousness of the news, gloating over every detail, and suggests that the Prince should practise for the interview with his father next morning. Thereupon he acts the part of the King rebuking the Prince, giving himself opportunity for plenty of 'hits' at the Prince and compliments for himself: then they change parts, which gives the Prince an opportunity to get his own back.

Meanwhile the law has not been idle. A hue and cry has 'followed certain men into this house', one of them (who could hardly hope to escape recognition) 'a gross fat man', and the Sheriff has come with the watch to search the house. The thieves hide, and the Prince gets rid of the Sheriff by telling a lie, and the Sheriff has to accept the word of the Prince of Wales.

The scene closes with the playing of another trick on Falstaff – picking his pockets as he lies asleep behind the arras, where he had gone into hiding.

fat vat (?).

lend me thy hand As we say, 'Give me a hand', i.e. help me.

base-string A metaphor from a stringed musical instrument. 'Base' = bass.

leash set of three hounds, hares, etc.

drawers barmen, tapsters (those who 'draw' the beer).

christen See note p.41.

take it upon their salvation will lay their salvation to it.

Corinthian 'gay dog.'

good Here used in the same sense as in 'a good sport'.

watering drinking.

play quaff.

tinker Tinkers were a byword for drunkenness and bad language.

under-skinker under-waiter or tapster.

Score enter on the bill.

bastard sweet Spanish wine.

Half-moon Name of a room in the tavern.

a precedent how to do it.

perfect i.e. in the way you do it.

Pomgarnet Pomegranate. Another room in the tavern.

to serve i.e. of his apprenticeship.

by'r lady by our Lady, i.e. the Virgin Mary.

books i.e. Bibles.

not-pated with hair cut short.

puke of a dark grey colour.

caddis worsted ribbon used for garters.

Spanish-pouch The aping of foreign fashions was a stock subject of Elizabethan satire.

Barbary There is no point in the Prince's remark—he cannot think of anything better to say to keep Francis.

match plot, trick. cf. note p.33. Poins evidently thought the Prince had something in mind—something more than met the eye – in the joke upon Francis.

humours See note p.35.

pupil age Now one word.

parcel of a reckoning items comprising a bill.

Hotspur Contrast the Prince's playful estimate of Hotspur with Hotspur's deep-seated contempt for the Prince (I. iii. 230–3). We are not allowed to forget the opposition of these two, even in the mirth of the tavern.

me Redundant.

drench dose of medicine.

brawn, ribs, tallow i.e. Falstaff. 'Ribs', of course, is sarcastic.

nether stocks stockings.

virtue manliness.

Titan Probably the Titan sun-god, Hyperion, is meant.

that Obviously refers to 'butter'.

lime Put in sack to make it keep longer.

forgot forgotten—commonly a past participle in Elizabethan English.

shotten spawned, and therefore worthless.

while times.

weaver . . . psalms A large proportion of London weavers in Shakespeare's time (not Henry IV's) consisted of Calvinist refugees from Flanders, who soon got a reputation for singing psalms at their work. Obviously, those Calvinists who gave up everything to start again in a foreign land were the most sincere – the others would conform to the state religion – and thus most likely to keep their religious habits.

dagger of lath Such as was carried by the Vice in the Morality plays, predecessors of Elizabethan drama. (More Elizabethan local colour.)

You Prince of Wales! The 'you' is emphatic, spoken with great contempt.

I'll see thee damned ... coward One way of getting out of a tight corner!

but I would give ... as thou canst He returns to his charge in more indirect language.

All's one for that it doesn't matter in spite of that.

A plague ... still say I Falstaff is longing for the Prince to ask what has happened, but, of course, the Prince doesn't 'bite' at first.

at half-sword with i.e. half a sword's length away from, at close quarters.

ecce signum 'behold the sign', a tag of Catholic ritual.

other others.

paid settled their score, finished them off.

ward See note p.35.

mainly with might and main.

target shield.

hilts Commonly used in the plural, where we should say 'hilt'.

Dost thou hear me, Hal! The previous speech of the Prince was an aside to Poins, and Falstaff thinks that the Prince is not attending to him.

mark Punning on the two meanings, (1) notice, (2) add up.

hose trunk hose, breeches. Poins puns on the other meaning of 'points' – braces (laces actually).

with a thought as quickly as one could think of it, on the instant, like lightning.

Kendal green Made at Kendal, Westmorland. Kendal green (like Lincoln green) was traditional foresters' dress.

clay-brained stupid, dull.

knotty-pated See note on 'not-pated', p.47.

ketch barrel.

strappado A form of torture which consisted in tying a rope round a person, or to his wrists, and alternately raising him by it and letting him go down quickly.

racks Instruments of torture by stretching.

sanguine red-faced.

starveling See note p.41. Falstaff retaliates on the Prince with 'comparisons' of thin things.

neat ox.

stock-fish fish cut into strips and dried in the sun.

yard i.e. yard measure.

standing-tuck rapier standing on end.

We two . . . Notice the number of monosyllables, which adds to the simplicity of the Prince's 'plain tale'.

out-faced frightened.

starting-hole hole in which to hide, to 'start' into as a way of escape.

Hercules Hero of Roman mythology, famed for his feats of strength.

beware take heed of.

argument See note p.43.

Ah, no more . . . me Falstaff worsted for once.

as much . . . royal man Punning on the coins, a noble, worth 34p, and a royal (also called a 'rose noble'), worth 50p.

spear-grass grass with stiff, pointed leaves.

true men i.e. the Travellers, not the thieves.

I blushed . . . devices Bardolph blames the others, particularly the one who is absent.

taken with the manner caught in the act.

thou hast blushed Alluding to Bardolph's red face.

meteors, exhalations Pointing to the spots on his face.

Hot livers and cold purses i.e. drunkenness and poverty.

choler Bardolph means that he will get angry if the Prince continues. By 'if rightly taken' he means 'if rightly understood'. The Prince puns on 'choler' and 'collar' (i.e. 'halter'), and uses Bardolph's word 'taken' in the sense of 'captured', as in 'taken with the manner', above.

bombast soft fibrous material for padding cushions, quilts, etc.

Amamon A demon.

Lucifer The Devil.

cross of a Welsh hook As a Christian swears by the Cross, so Glendower made the devil swear to be his true liegeman on a Welsh hook!

pistol Another example of Elizabethan local colour.

blue-caps i.e. Scots.

state chair of state.

joined-stool folding stool.

King Cambyses' vein There was a play on the life of King Cambises of Persia. The audience would no doubt appreciate the allusion. Evidently the part of the King was a ranting part.

leg i.e. bow.

Weep not etc. This and Falstaff's next speech are 'in King Cambyses' vein' – bombast.

holds his countenance i.e. stops himself from laughing, keeps his face serious.

tristful sad.

harlotry A juggler or buffoon was called a 'harlot' in Elizabethan times, without any imputation of the modern meaning.

tickle-brain one who deals in strong liquor.

micher truant.

naughty good-for-nothing—a much stronger word than now.

varlet rascal.

rabbit-sucker suckling rabbit.

poulter poulterer.

nay, I'll . . . i' faith An aside to the onlookers.

bolting-hutch tub for sifted flour or meal.

bombard large drinking-vessel.

cloak-bag a bag in which a cloak or other clothes were carried.

Manningtree ox A famous fair was held annually at Manningtree, Essex, one of the attractions of which was the roasting of a whole ox.

cunning skilful. cf. *Psalm* CXXXVII. 5, 'Let my right hand forget her *cunning*' (skill).

take me with you enlighten me; allow me to 'come in', as we say.

Pharaoh's lean kine See *Genesis* XLI. 1–4, 25–31.

Dost thou hear, Hal? Falstaff is annoyed at having his apology for himself interrupted, and is here 'playing out the play' in spite of everything. He himself, of course, is the 'true piece of gold'.

major major premise in argument, from which all the rest follows.

so all well and good.

cart i.e. hangman's cart.

arras tapestry, so called because originally made at Arras, in the north of France. cf. 'Kendal green', note p.49.

true face i.e. such a face as is possessed by a 'true man'.

their date is out Metaphor from coinage no longer current.

Peto. Is this a mistake for 'Poins'? Poins was the only one beside the Prince not concerned in the robbery of the Travellers, and therefore the only one besides him not likely to go into hiding. In any case there is no need for Poins to hide.

by to-morrow dinner-time See p.10.

marks See note p.41.

Paul's St. Paul's Cathedral.

ob obulus, a halfpenny.

close secret. cf. note p.43.

more advantage a better opportunity.

place position, office. The Prince is going to use his influence to advance the fortunes of his friends.

charge of foot command ('charge') of infantry.

twelve-score i.e. feet or yards.

advantage interest.

Revision questions on Act II

1 Describe a typical Elizabethan inn-yard scene in the early morning, basing your description on Scene i.

2 What do you gather of Hotspur's home-life from Scene iii?

3 State how on three occasions Falstaff gets out of a tight corner by his nimble wit.

4 Describe the practical jokes played on Falstaff in this Act.

5 What impression of Prince Hal are you given by the scene in the Boar's Head Tavern?

Act III Scene i

The rebel leaders meet to formulate their plans. At the outset the peace and harmony of the meeting is imperilled by Hotspur, who openly makes fun of Glendower's pretensions to magic powers. Shrewsbury is appointed the meeting-place of the rebel forces. The rebels plan to divide England and Wales into three parts, to be assigned to Mortimer, Glendower and Hotspur respectively. Hotspur squabbles like a spoilt child because his share appears less than that of the others, and then when he gets his own way adds insult to injury by saying that it does not matter, he protested only for the sake of argument. It takes all the patience of Mortimer and Worcester to bear with him. It is no credit to him that things are smoothed over: on each occasion it is Glendower who gives way before his aggressiveness.

Glendower goes to inform the ladies of the imminent departure of their husbands and bring them in for a farewell social gathering. While he is away Mortimer and Worcester remonstrate with Hotspur for his behaviour. At the gathering there is music and singing. Hotspur thinks music a waste of time and (somewhat to the embarrassment of his wife) talks while it is in progress and mimics the sentimental doting on one another of the two newly-weds, Mortimer and his wife. Here again he makes himself a nuisance, though certainly we would not be without his mimicry.

See also p.4.

induction start, preliminaries.

a plague ... map Typical of the headstrong Hotspur. cf. note on 'what ... place', p.38. For 'forgot', see note p.48.

For Implying 'I add your nickname because ...'

Lancaster Not the Lancaster of the play, but Henry IV, who was heir to the dukedom of Lancaster before he won the crown by deposing Richard II. In fact when he first landed he said it was to claim only his dukedom of Lancaster. Glendower refers to him by the title to which he has a right, and not that of king, to which he has no right.

cressets vessels holding oil for lights, mounted on poles.

Why ... born Why is this speech in prose?

enlargement freedom.

topples Here used transitively.

distemperature disorder.

passion pain, suffering.

these crossings such opposition, thwarting.

clipp'd in with surrounded by.

Which Really 'who': the antecedent is 'he'.

read to i.e. taught. cf. a 'reader' at a University.

deep i.e. magic. 'Art' also has the sense of 'magic art'.

vasty vast.

But will ... them? A delightful rejoinder, although tactless in these circumstances.

head opposition, resistance.

weather-beaten Implying that he conjured up the bad weather to harass the king.

Come, here's the map When all is said and done, Glendower is fairly good-natured (if not 'wondrous affable'). It is he who first gives way and turns to business, letting Hotspur have the last word.

right what we have a right to, i.e. the land.

hitherto to this place. He is pointing on the map.

drawn drawn up.

sealed interchangeably each indenture bearing the seals of all three.

Within . . . gentlemen Mortimer speaks this turning to Glendower. Glendower would naturally need longer than the others to assemble his forces, owing to the difficult nature of his country.

moiety share, lit. 'half' (Fr. 'moitié')

cranking bending. The 'me' is redundant.

cantle piece, slice.

smug smooth. Notice the beauty and exactness of the adjectives applied to rivers in this play. Glendower speaks of the 'sandy-bottom'd Severn' earlier in the scene, and see also I. iii. 103–6.

bottom valley. Still so used in the West Riding of Yorkshire.

he i.e. the river.

Gelding the opposed continent taking away from the land on the bank opposite.

charge See note p.30.

I can speak English . . . in you Glendower has no sense of humour. He takes Hotspur's remark here as a slight upon his speaking of English.

And I am glad . . . This is spoken by a man whose nature is deeply imaginative. See pp.15–6.

canstick candlestick.

turn'd i.e. on a lathe.

nothing not at all.

Come . . . turn'd Anything for a minute's peace! It is Glendower who gives way a second time.

I do not care See p.52.

writer copyist of the indentures.

Break with inform, as in '*break* the news'.

moldwarp mole.

Merlin Magician of the Arthurian legends.

moulten háving moulted.

couching couchant, lying down with head raised. A heraldic term.

ramping rampant, rearing. Another heraldic term.

skimble-skamble rambling.

faith i.e. faith or trust in him.

several separate, i.e. each one with a separate name.

cates delicacies. The word still survives in 'to cater' and 'caterer'.

profited in strange concealments proficient in secret magic studies and practices.

temper temperament.

Might who might.

wilful-blame wilfully making yourself to blame.

blood spirit, dash.

dearest greatest. In Elizabethan English one could have a 'dear friend' and a 'dear enemy'. cf. 'dear expedience', note p.30.

government self-control.

opinion being opinionated.

hearts i.e. approval.

them The beautiful 'parts'.

father Actually father-in-law. cf. l.87.

Aunt Historically sister.

harlotry See note p.51. Here the meaning is that she gives exaggerated expression to her feelings.

these swelling heavens The metaphor identifies the tears in her eyes with the rain from the 'heavens'.

such a parley such language, i.e. tears.

feeling disputation a conversation of feelings—as opposed to one of words.

highly elaborately.

division music.

melt Referring to Mortimer's 'but for shame, in such a parley should I answer thee'.

this i.e. the meaning of the Welsh.

wanton luxuriant.

heavenly harness'd team the team of horses harnessed to the chariot of the sun.

book the indentures.

humorous moody. See note on 'humour', p.35.

brach bitch.

still quiet.

Neither i.e. neither would I be 'still'.

comfit sweetmeat.

sarcenet thin. Sarcenet is a fine silk, so called because originally made by the Saracens.

pepper-gingerbread Such as might be made by a 'comfit-maker's wife'.

velvet-guards people with velvet trimmings on their dress.

Sunday-citizens i.e. dressed in their 'Sunday best'.

next See note p.41.

tailor Tailors, like weavers, were supposed to sing at their work.

seal i.e. seal the indentures – 'interchangeably', as agreed.

Act III Scene ii

This is the interview between the King and the Prince which had been played over in fun the night before at the tavern. It proceeds something as follows.

King. I wonder whether my having such a son is heaven's scourge for my 'mistreadings'.

Prince. I would I could clear myself of all offences as easily as I can many of those with which I am charged. As I refute charges which are malicious inventions, so may I find pardon for my real faults on my true submission.

King. May God pardon thee! (i.e. His pardon, not mine, you need.)

I obtained the throne by keeping myself aloof from the common people, so that I appeared remarkable to them when I *was* seen.

Richard lost the throne by mixing with them, so that they took no notice of him.

You are just like him.

Prince. In future I will be more what I ought to be.

King. You appear to the world just as Richard did when I landed as a rebel, and Hotspur appears as I did. (The implication is obvious, that Hotspur is likely to get more public support than the Prince.) You are 'like enough to fight against me under Percy's pay'.

Prince. I will conquer Percy, and so all his glories shall come to me, or else

> the end of life cancels all bands;
> And I will die a hundred thousand deaths
> Ere break the smallest parcel of this vow.

King (convinced of the Prince's loyalty by his last speech). 'A hundred thousand rebels die in this.' You shall have a command in my army.

Notice in detail the King's account of how he gained the throne (ll.39–59) and how Richard lost it (ll.60–84), and also the contrast he develops between Hotspur and the Prince (ll.97–118).

Blunt brings the news that Douglas and the English rebels have successfully met at Shrewsbury, but the King says that he has known of it for five days, and outlines his plans for joining his forces at Bridgenorth to oppose them.

give us leave A polite way of saying 'Take your leave.'
presently See note p.41.
blood offspring.
revengement revenge.
passages ways.
lewd base, worthless.
blood descent, family.
Quit be rid of.
reproof See note p.35.
pick-thanks flatterers.
newsmongers tell-tales.
By Preposition after 'devised'.
true i.e. where the faults laid to my charge are true.
hold a wing Metaphor from hawking.
from away from.
thy time i.e. when you will succeed to the throne.
do Because the idea of 'every man' (thought of as 'all men') is plural.
opinion i.e. public opinion.
possession the one in possession. Abstract for concrete, as often in
  Elizabethan English.

likelihood promise.

courtesy from heaven His courtesy was as great as if it came from heaven.

pontifical belonging to the Pope or a bishop.

wan won.

solemnity ceremony.

bavin a bundle of brushwood for kindling a fire—with the application which follows in the next line.

carded 'mingled'.

against his name to the injury of his name as king.

stand . . . comparative bear the retort of every boy vain enough to match his wit against that of the king.

Enfeoff'd gave up.

a little more . . . much too much even a *little* too much cloys as much as a surfeit.

community familiarity, lit. commonness.

in his face before his very eyes.

cloudy i.e. threatening.

vile participation participation in vile things.

foolish tenderness i.e. tears.

I shall . . . myself The Prince's few simple words make us feel the sincerity of his promise. They stand in marked contrast to his father's long speech.

Ravenspurgh See note p.39.

to boot as well.

He hath . . . succession i.e. the Prince's claim to the throne by being first in the line of succession is like a shadow before the real worth of Hotspur for the position, and Hotspur has more right to the throne than the Prince has to this mere shadow.

of by.

colour misrepresentation, false appearance – a colour which disguises a real appearance. cf. the use as a verb, p.37.

harness armour. Metonymy.

the lion i.e. the King.

arms weapons.

Holds . . . majority all soldiers hold it as their opinion that he excels all others. For 'holds' as a singular verb, cf. 'do', above.

capital chief, he is at the head of them all.

Mars Roman god of war.

swathling swaddling.

ta'en i.e. captive.

Enlarged freed.

To fill . . . defiance up to defy me fully.

Capitulate draw up terms or grievances under heads.

up i.e. in arms.

dearest See note p.55.

like See note p.34.

vassal low, base.

start impulse.

favours face, features.

lights chances to come.

engross up amass.

worship honour.

bands bonds.

parcel part.

charge i.e. of men.

eleventh of this month Notice the sense of reality given by the circumstantial detail again. See note on 'on Wednesday next. Windsor', p.31.

head See note p.39.

advertisement news.

Wednesday. Thursday See note on 'eleventh of this month', above.

meeting meeting-place.

valued rightly estimated.

Our hands are full of business we have plenty to do.

Advantage opportunity. As in the first note on the word, p.52.

feeds him fat And thus deteriorates (gets unable to take his chance) by growing slothful. 'Him' = himself.

Act III Scene iii

In an introductory part to the main scene (cf. II. iv. p.43) Bardolph makes fun of Falstaff's fatness, and Falstaff retaliates at the expense of Bardolph's red face. The Hostess enters, and Falstaff asks her if the person who picked his pocket has been found out, but the Hostess accuses him of inventing the pocket-picking, so as to cheat her of her reckoning. Falstaff says that he

has lost a ring 'worth forty mark' and upon the Hostess's declaring that many a time the Prince has told him the ring was
copper, Falstaff says he would cudgel the Prince if he said so.

At that moment the Prince and Peto come in. Falstaff adds
'three or four bonds of forty pounds a-piece' to what has been
taken from his pocket. The Hostess tries to get the Prince on her
side against Falstaff, and tells him that Falstaff said the other
day that the Prince owed him 'a thousand pound'. Falstaff's
nimble wit is never at a loss. 'A thousand pound, Hal!' he says,
'a million: thy love is worth a million: thou owest me thy love.'
The Hostess follows this up by telling the Prince of Falstaff's
threat to cudgel him if he said his ring was copper. 'I say 'tis
copper,' says the Prince, whereupon Falstaff (as in II. iv) falls
back on the Prince's position, and replies,

Why, Hal, thou knowest, as thou art but man, I dare: but as thou art
prince, I fear thee as I fear the roaring of the lion's whelp.

When another 'plain tale' is told by the Prince of what really
was in Falstaff's pocket, Falstaff, never beaten, has his excuse
ready.

Thou knowest in the state of innocency Adam fell; and what should
poor Jack Falstaff do in the days of villany? Thou seest I have more
flesh than another man, and therefore more frailty.

He then says that he *forgives* the Hostess (as if *she* had anything
to be forgiven for!). Compare the ways Falstaff gets out of the
scrapes that his lies get him into in this scene with those in
Act II Scene iv.

The Prince announces that he has procured a command of
infantry for Falstaff and gives orders to Bardolph and Peto
concerning the mobilization. Even though it is a scene of tavern
merry-making, it ends in a business-like and dashing tone.
There is serious work for *everyone* to do. The change is accompanied by a change from prose to verse.

am I not fallen away have I not lost flesh?
bate abate, 'fall away'.

apple-john A kind of apple said to taste best when it has been kept two years and its skin is all wrinkled.

in some liking in the mood for it.

peppercorn A humorous comparison, a peppercorn is so small.

brewer's horse To be called a 'malt-horse' was considered an insult in Shakespeare's time.

been the spoil of spoilt.

in good compass with moderation. Bardolph puns on the word, using it in reference to Falstaff's size.

admiral flag-ship.

Death's-head skull (as an emblem of mortality).

memento mori 'remember that you must die' (Lat.).

Dives See *Luke*, XVI. 19–31.

that A relative pronoun.

given over lost, i.e. to virtue.

wert would be.

ignis fatuus will-o'-the-wisp.

purchase purchasing power.

triumph show, spectacle, celebration (with fireworks, bonfires and torches), a triumph in the Roman sense – the ceremony in honour of a triumph.

links torches of pitch and tow, used for lighting people's way along streets.

hast drunk me hast drunk at my expense.

chandler candle-maker (or seller).

salamander In medieval times, a fabulous animal supposed to live in fire. Falstaff means that he has maintained the fire in Bardolph's face by providing him with liquor. The real salamander is a brightly-coloured lizard-like creature.

God-a-mercy! Corruption of 'God have mercy!'

Partlet A name often applied to a hen, e.g. in Chaucer's *Nonnes Preestes Tale*.

God's light Did this escape the censor? See note on ' 'Sblood', p.33.

Dowlas A strong coarse linen.

bolters sieves. See note on 'bolting-hutch', p.51.

holland linen material.

ell an old measure of forty-five inches in length.

by-drinkings drinks not taken with a meal or 'diet'.

denier A French coin of trifling value. The modern equivalent of what Falstaff says is 'I'll not pay a cent.'

younker dupe.

Jack rascal.

sneak-cup lit. one who is afraid to take a good drink from a cup, who sneaks sips.

door cf. our idiom substituting 'quarter' for 'door'.

Newgate A prison.

Wilt thou believe me, Hal? Why does Falstaff feel the need of this preface?

drawn i.e. from its hole, and therefore cringing.

Maid Marian The original Maid Marian became the wife of Robin Hood. A player representing Maid Marian was invariably included in May Day celebrations, a natural association in view of the scene of most of the Robin Hood stories – 'under the greenwood tree'. The 'Maid Marians' of Shakespeare's time, however, had the reputation of being undesirable women.

deputy's wife of the ward to thee wife of the deputy (i.e. deputy sheriff's officer) of the ward (district in a town) compared to you. The deputy's wife would be a respectable woman with a reputation to uphold, and what Falstaff says is that the Hostess is a woman of such very low character that Maid Marian would be considered respectable by the side of her.

where to have her how to classify her ('fish or flesh').

ought owed.

Did I, Bardolph? Said, no doubt, hoping Bardolph would deny it.

midriff guts, lit. diaphragm.

embossed swollen.

injuries things which would be a loss if taken.

pocket up wrong Used in the sense of our 'swallow an insult'. The pun on 'pocket up' is obvious.

pacified made peaceable, disposed to make peace.

still See note p.39.

with unwashed hands i.e. without waiting a moment.

charge See note p.59.

foot infantry.

I laud them The reason Falstaff praises the rebels is that they have brought him a position he would otherwise never have had.

temple Probably one of the Inns of Court.
furniture equipment.
drum i.e. recruiting depot. Proclamations concerning recruiting
were preceded by a roll of the drum.

Revision questions on Act III

1 Describe how Hotspur nearly wrecks the rebels' council-
meeting.

2 What are the rebels' plans (a) for the battle against the King,
(b) for the division of the land after the victory they hope for?

3 Do you sympathise with Hotspur's behaviour at the farewell
party after the council-meeting?

4 Recount in detail and in due order the conversation between
the King and the Prince of Wales at their private interview. Add
a few comments on the Prince's bearing.

5 State how on three occasions in Scene iii Falstaff gets out of
the predicaments that his lies have got him into. What simi-
larities are there to his evasions in Act II Scene iv?

Act IV Scene i
The misfortunes of the rebels increase apace. News is brought
that Northumberland is sick and cannot join them. At first
Worcester and Hotspur are both taken aback, but in the next
breath Hotspur's will to succeed makes a virtue of necessity and
interprets bad news as good. Should we fail, he says, Northumberland's forces are in reserve, and so we have a second line
of defence to fall back upon; further, the fewer we are the
greater the honour in our enterprise. Worcester, however, can
see no good in the news. He says little in front of Hotspur, but it
is quite evident he thinks Northumberland's sickness is just an
excuse, and when he says that folks will think Northumberland
keeps away for fear, it is obviously what he himself thinks, but
he disguises it like this out of respect for Hotspur's feelings for
his father.

Misfortunes seldom come singly. Vernon brings news of the

enemy's strength and their own weakness. In answer to a question of Hotspur as to the whereabouts of the Prince, Vernon pays the Prince a glowing tribute in a picturesque and colourful description of his setting out. This irritates Hotspur, and shows him up in contrast to the Prince, who is ever ready to acknowledge merit in Hotspur. Hotspur's one ambition is to meet the Prince in the battle.

> Harry to Harry shall, hot horse to horse,
> Meet and ne'er part till one drop down a corse.

Vernon keeps the worst news until last. Glendower cannot come for fourteen days. To Worcester this 'bears a frosty sound', and even Hotspur, in spite of brave words, ends the scene talking of 'doomsday' and dying.

fine showy.

attribution tribute.

stamp . . . current A metaphor from currency again. See notes on pp.36, 41 and 45. The meaning is that in this age no one would be regarded as such a true soldier – such a *genuine* one – as Douglas.

soothers flatterers, people who say *soothing* things.

braver finer, higher. cf. p.33.

task me to put me to, take me at.

approve See note p.31.

No man . . . beard him Douglas shows no signs of modesty. He does, it is true, return Hotspur's praise, but at the same time he sings his own praises. 'Beard' = tackle, oppose, defy.

justling jostling.

fear'd feared for.

state of time condition of affairs.

whole well (in health).

better worth of more value.

catching Continuing the metaphor of an infectious disease.

sickness— Hotspur is too agitated to finish this sentence. Further, he must be imagined as continuing to read the letter.

deputation a deputy.

drawn drawn together.

removed other than his own.

advertisement advice.

conjunction joint forces.

is possess'd of has knowledge of.

maim Now only used as a verb. Here a noun.

his present want our need of him now.

To set . . . cast? to stake the limit of our fortunes on one throw (leaving nothing in reserve) ?

main hand of cards (Fr. 'main' = hand).

nice precarious.

list . bound limit, boundary.

Where whereas.

reversion something to which one expects to succeed – 'the hope of what is to come in' (a legal term).

spend i.e. use our men.

upon relying upon, on the strength of.

retirement something to fall back on.

rendezvous meeting-place.

maidenhead first part. cf. *maiden* speech, *maiden* voyage.

hair complexion, nature.

wisdom i.e. for his own safety.

offering offensive, attacking.

stop stop up.

loop loophole.

draws i.e. draws aside.

larger dare greater daring.

Yet up to now.

No harm there is no harm in that.

intended intends (to set forth).

daff'd put aside (another form of 'doff').

furnish'd equipped. See note on 'furniture', p.63.

estridges goshawks.

Bated having ruffled plumage. Used of falcons, hawks, etc.

like images i.e. decked for a festival.

beaver helmet, strictly speaking the lower face-guard of the helmet.

cuisses armour for the thighs.

Mercury Roman messenger of the gods, usually represented with winged ankles, hence 'feather'd'.

Pegasus A winged horse of Greek mythology.

witch bewitch.

in their trim i.e. decked for sacrifice.
maid of smoky war Goddess of war – Bellona to the Romans.
Mars See note p.59.
reprisal that which is taken in reprisal, prize.
taste test.
battle army, forces for battle, 'power'.
serve serve for, be sufficient for.

Act IV Scene ii

The Prince has been as good as his word and procured Falstaff 'a charge of foot', but Falstaff has misused damnably the king's commission to levy soldiers. He conscripted none but men of substance and those who would particularly want to be exempt, such as those about to get married, cowards and those who disliked roughing it. These people, therefore, bought out their services, and Falstaff filled their places with pitiful unemployed rascals and rogues just out of prison. In this way he made three hundred pounds. Nevertheless, he will not give money to Bardolph to go and fetch him some sack, telling him to get it on credit. Falstaff dwells on his cleverness and gloats over the raggedness of his scarecrow company.

The Prince and Westmoreland come across him on the road near Coventry. Falstaff is thick-skinned enough to jest before them about his beggarly soldiers, and says that his 'pitiful rascals' are ' good enough to toss; food for powder, food for powder; they'll fill a pit as well as better'.

get thee before go on in front.
Sutton Co'fil' Sutton Coldfield, in Warwickshire, near Birmingham.
lay out i.e. credit.
makes i.e. with what we are in debt up to now.
angel In full 'angel noble' (cf. note on 'as much . . . royal man', p.50), a coin worth 34p in the fifteenth century, and about 50p at the time of Shakespeare, so called because it was stamped with a design of the archangel Michael piercing a dragon.
gurnet A kind of sea-fish with a large head.
press power to conscript ('press') men for my army. Used as a verb in the speech. (cf. 'impressed', note p.30.)

contracted engaged to be married.

commodity collection.

warm passionately in love.

lieve soon.

caliver an early form of hand gun.

struck i.e. wounded by a bullet.

toasts-and-butter self-indulgent people—people whose fare included toast and butter.

ancients ensigns.

gentlemen of companies corresponding to sub-lieutenants.

Lazarus See *Luke*, XVI. 19–21. cf. note on 'Dives', p.61.

painted cloth tapestry.

discarded dismissed, 'sacked'.

unjust dishonest.

younger ... brothers Consequently unable to get a living out of the family business as the family grew.

revolted having left their work.

trade-fallen unemployed owing to bad times. Notice the different reasons for their being out of work which Falstaff particularizes in this sentence.

canker See note p.38.

faced patched up (?). To 'face' a garment is to cover or line it with a different material, usually for ornament.

draff refuse, pig-swill.

gyves fetters.

St. Alban's A small town in Hertfordshire, twenty miles north-west of London.

Daventry A small town in Northamptonshire, about twelve miles south-east of Rugby.

on every hedge i.e. hung out to dry.

blown i.e. blown up like a balloon.

cry you mercy ask your pardon. In his surprise and joy at seeing the Prince he evidently ignores Westmoreland.

looks for expects.

away keep on the way.

toss i.e. on a pike.

pit grave.

three fingers i.e. three fingers' thickness of fat.

the latter end of a fray Falstaff, 'a dull fighter and a keen guest', implies that he hopes he *does* arrive too late for the fight.

Act IV Scene iii

The armies now face one another near Shrewsbury, the night before the battle. Hotspur wants to attack straight away, while the King's horses are tired and before his supplies come up, and Douglas supports him, seemingly for no other reason than that Hotspur advises it. Worcester and Vernon, on the other hand, counsel tarrying until the morrow, as their own horses are tired and they themselves no less look for reinforcements. As we should expect from Act III Scene i, Hotspur will not give way, and Douglas has not the intelligence to grasp other people's reasons and thinks counsel with which he does not agree is the result of fear, and says so.

Tempers are thus frayed and things are working up to a quarrel, when Sir Walter Blunt enters with generous peace terms from the King, offering redress for the rebels' grievances and full pardon. Hotspur replies that they know from experience what the King's promises are like, and reiterates their grievances, which he has already enumerated in Act I Scene iii. (Without consulting his colleagues) Hotspur says that they will think over the King's offers and Worcester shall bring a reply in the morning.

Thus the question when to attack, which was the subject at issue at the beginning of the scene, is settled for them by the entry of Sir Walter Blunt, as they now decide to defer an answer on the King's terms till morning.

At this point it would be well to consider the ill-omens gathering like clouds round the rebels' cause. Northumberland is half-hearted from the first (I. i. 300) and drops out in Act IV Scene i. His defection is the more serious in view of Glendower's inability to come in time (IV. i). The rebels cannot agree in council in the early stages (III. i) or even the night before the battle. In Act IV Scene iv we see that one of their chief supporters fears their defeat and is making arrangements accordingly *before the battle has been fought*.

Notice how, on each occasion when Shakespeare makes us

feel disgusted with the rebels or realize the hopelessness of their cause, he quickly gives us reason to transfer the sympathy they have lost to the King's side. Act III Scene i, where the rebels quarrel among themselves and carve up the land according to their fancy, without any thoughts for the national welfare now or peace in the future, is followed by the scene where the Prince increases in our favour by his bearing before his father. The ominous news of Northumberland's defection is immediately succeeded by Vernon's description of the promise of the Prince as he set out for battle (IV. i). On the heels of the quarrel in this scene comes the King's 'gracious offer'. We are not left with sympathy 'in vacuum', so to speak. Immediately it is taken away from one side we have good cause to place it on the other.

well-respected well thought out beforehand (as opposed to rash actions).

leading leadership.

expedition The same meaning as 'expedience', see note p.30.

horse i.e. cavalry.

is asleep A singular verb because 'pride and mettle' are thought of collectively. cf. note on 'agrees', p.34.

journey-bated worn out with their journey.

quality side.

defend forbid.

limit the bounds of the constitution.

charge task, duty, that which I am 'charged' to do.

griefs grievances.

whereupon wherefore.

strong i.e. in number of his followers.

unminded nobody took any notice of him.

but only.

sue his livery claim the dukedom to which he was heir.

more and less greater and less people (in social position).

with cap and knee taking off their caps and kneeling before him.

knows becomes conscious of.

blood See note p.55.

certain specified, particular ones.

strait oppressive, lit. narrowing.

face appearance.

deputation See note p.54.

personal personally taking part.

in the neck of immediately following. A racing metaphor.

task'd taxed.

engaged held as a hostage.

intelligence spies. Abstract for concrete, as often in Elizabethan English.

Rated . . . board. See Act I, Sc. iii.

of i.e. for our.

to pry i.e. drove us to pry.

impawn'd pledged.

Act IV Scene iv

The Archbishop of York, one of the supporters of the rebellion, is despatching letters arranging for those of the confederates left 'to make strong against' the King, assuming that he wins the battle of Shrewsbury.

From the 'to-morrow' in l.8 it is evident that the scene takes place on the same day as the previous scene.

This scene adds nothing to the plot or to our knowledge of any of the characters. It does, however, give a growing sense of the hopelessness of the rebels' cause.

brief letter. cf. a barrister's *briefs* in law.

How . . . import how important they are.

bide the touch be put to the test.

o'er-ruled by prophecies Notice this reason for Glendower's absence, in addition to the one given by Vernon in Sc. ii. Which do you think is the right one?

moe more.

corrivals See note p.38. Here they are competitors for honour.

his power i.e. his own 'power' (not Lord Percy's).

Revision questions on Act IV

1 What is the bad news received by the rebels in Scene i? How does (a) Hotspur, (b) Worcester regard it?

2 How did Falstaff make 'three hundred and odd pounds' for himself in recruiting his company?

3 What are the reasons of (1) Hotspur and Douglas for advising immediate battle, (b) Worcester and Vernon for advising delay till morning?

4 What is the dramatic purpose of Scene iv?

Act V Scene i
The King interprets the weather on the morning of the battle as a bad omen for the rebels (a touch of sympathetic background).

As Hotspur promised (IV. iii), Worcester, accompanied by Vernon, comes to the King on behalf of the rebels. Worcester repeats the grievances of the rebels; the King says that they are but excuses for rebellion, but renews his offers of peace and redress.

Meanwhile the Prince has offered to settle the quarrel by single-combat with Hotspur, in order 'to save blood on either side'. The Prince's challenge is set off by his generous praise of Hotspur, together with modest self-depreciation. He shows that his promise to his father in Act III Scene ii was not a promise of empty words. The Prince and Hotspur now have one desire – to meet each other in fight (see IV. i. 119–23, and p.64).

By this time Falstaff has arrived at Shrewsbury, intent as ever on saving his own skin. The scene ends with his famous catechism on honour.

busky bushy.

At his distemperature by the side of, in contrast with his (the sun's) sickly look.

play the trumpet As a herald, announcing what sort of day it is going to be.

orb orbit.

exhaled Meteors were supposed to be caused by exhalations of the vapours of the earth. A meteor is a temporary phenomenon, with no regular course like a planet, and hence stands in antithesis with 'orbit'.

broached let loose. Metaphor from broaching a cask.

unborn i.e. future.

entertain spend.

chewet chough, i.e. chatter-box.

remember remind.

my staff . . . break Worcester resigned the office of steward of the king's household.

posted See note p.30.

outdare face, defy.

new-fall'n On account of the death of his father.

the absent king the absence of the king. See IV. iii. 88.

sufferances sufferings.

woo'd . . . sway persuaded to seize absolute power.

gull young bird. The cuckoo is noted for its habit of laying its eggs in the nests of other birds, instead of building one of its own. When the young cuckoo, thus hatched by a foster-parent, grows up, it displaces those who have a rightful claim to the nest.

swallowing being swallowed.

such means . . . against yourself i.e. you are to blame for this opposition against you, as by your own actions you yourself have forced us to rebellion.

dangerous countenance a bearing threatening danger (to us).

younger enterprise His original intention to gain his dukedom only.

articulate articulated.

face See note p.70.

changelings turncoats.

discontents discontented people.

rub the elbow A way of showing pleasure in a crowd.

want lack.

water-colours The same idea of a surface attractiveness as 'face' above. That it is only surface is emphasized by 'water-colours' which are not so enduring as those in oil. Cf. note on 'colour', p.58.

starving See note p.36.

for for the lack of, or till the coming of.

confusion ruin.

by my hopes (I swear) by what I hope for.

set off his head not laid to his charge.

this this I state.

venture stake, engage.

Albeit See note p.37.

your cousin i.e. Hotspur.

Rebuke punishment.

wait on us are our attendants (for *us* to use against *you*).

both together in alliance.

bestride i.e. to defend me.

with . . . me as to pay a debt to a person who does not ask for it.

prick me off carry me off, i.e. kill me.

set to a leg set a (broken) leg.

grief See note p.36.

is insensible fails to make any impression on the bodily senses (e.g. feeling or hearing).

detraction will not suffer it slander will not allow it (to live).

scutcheon shield with armorial bearings. Probably here just a coat of arms is meant, i.e. honour is a mere decoration.

Act V Scene ii

The supreme act of treachery in the play is committed in this scene. Worcester decides not to disclose to Hotspur the 'liberal and kind offer of the king', made in the previous scene, and Vernon agrees, though unwillingly, to be his accomplice. Worcester thinks that if peace is made now the King will forgive a young fire-brand like Hotspur, but be on the watch to avenge himself on the older conspirators at the slightest pretext. He therefore tells Hotspur that the King will attack at once.

Worcester does, however, make known the Prince's challenge to Hotspur, and when Hotspur suggests that it was made in contempt, Vernon (perhaps feeling the impulse to make some amends for his acquiescence in Worcester's lie) is only too ready to do the Prince full justice.

The rebels prepare for battle.

punish . . . faults make other subsequent faults an excuse for punishing us for this one.

eyes i.e. ever on the watch for finding us out.

how however.

or sad or either seriously or.

misquote misread.

adopted name of privilege nickname that does him credit, or gives him an advantage over other people.

A hare-brain'd . . . spleen An excellent epitome of Hotspur's disposition.

live upon my head i.e. I am held to be responsible for them.

train entice.

Deliver . . . Westmoreland Westmoreland was the hostage for the safe return of Worcester and Vernon (see IV. iii. 108–11).

Defy him by i.e. let him take the message of defiance.

no seeming mercy nothing like mercy.

forswearing . . . forsworn by denying that he ever broke his word. 'Mended' is, of course, sarcastic.

engaged See note p.70.

draw short breath i.e. as a result of exertion. Notice that both Hotspur and the Prince have one desire, to meet each other in fight.

Harry Monmouth The Prince was born at Monmouth. See note on 'Bolingbroke', p.37.

tasking challenging.

I never . . . modestly See V. i. 83–100.

duties of qualities expected of.

Trimm'd up i.e. with praise that was not strictly necessary.

dispraising . . . you saying that he could not find words to praise you highly enough. 'Valued with' = compared with.

cital recital.

truant The very word used by the Prince (V. i. 94).

teaching and of learning teaching others (who were following in the footsteps of his 'truant youth') and of learning himself (from his own experience of it).

envy malice.

owe own, possess (the opposite of the meaning now).

misconstrued misinterpreted.

Cousin . . . libertine Hotspur is the one who speaks 'in contempt'!

embrace . . . courtesy The meeting in the battle, sarcastically spoken of with the terms one would apply to a friendly meeting.

Better . . . persuasion you can raise your spirits more by considering for yourselves what you have to do than I, who have not the gift of powerful oratory, can by exhorting you.

I cannot read them now It is quite in keeping with Hotspur's impetuous nature that he will not stop to read letters just at a time when they may be of supreme importance. The news in letters brought now might easily turn the scales of the battle. As it is he spends as long talking about the shortness of time as it would have taken him to read the letters.

To spend . . . long Even a short life (lasting only an hour) would be too long to be spent basely.

dial i.e. sundial.

for as for.

intent of motive for, purpose of.

just right.

I profess not talking I do not profess to be a talker. This from Hotspur!

Esperance See note p.45.

heaven to earth i.e. I stake heaven to earth.

Act V Scene iii

The stage cannot show a whole battle-field, but it can give the *impression* of a battle by showing a corner of that battle-field and also letting the fighters there refer to battle fortunes on other parts of the front. That is the function of this scene. A sense of hurry and breathlessness is given by the comings and goings of combatants on either side.

Douglas kills Blunt, thinking he is the King – the second he has killed that day dressed in the King's uniform. After a word of praise for his valour, Hotspur tells him who it is and that the King 'hath many marching in his coats'.

The Prince meets Falstaff, who offers him a bottle of sack when he needs his pistol. For once the Prince does not relish the joke: there is a time for joking and a time for seriousness.

A sense of the power of the rebels is given by the overcoming of Blunt by Douglas. This gives the impression now that to conquer them will not be easy, and makes the victory over them later seem a greater one. The harder the conflict the more glorious the triumph.

me i.e. my path.

Upon my head? at my expense?

They tell thee true Blunt is a 'true, industrious friend' to the last. See also pp.18–19.

Semblably furnish'd like equipped in a similar manner to. 'Semblably' and 'like' have the same meaning. For 'furnish'd', see note p.65.

his coats uniform or armour like his own.

shot-free scot-free.

scoring The sort of 'scoring' to which Falstaff was accustomed (which he puns on here) was that of a tavern reckoning.

there's honour for you Reverting to his catechism on honour.

here's no vanity Sarcasm.

to beg during life i.e. they are maimed.

Whose Antecedent 'Many a nobleman.'

breathe See note p.37.

Turk Gregory Hildebrand, who became Pope Gregory VII (1073–85).

pierce A pun with 'Percy', pronounced similarly.

so well and good.

carbonado rasher.

grinning honour i.e. in death. Still harking back to his catechism.

Act V Scene iv

The battle is continued, and in it the Prince 'redeems his lost opinion'. Everything redounds to his honour and glory.

1 His father, having seen his prowess, is at one with him. Notice the difference between the King's address to the Prince and that to his second son.

> *Harry*, withdraw *thyself*; *thou* bleed'st too much. (Familiar.)
> *Lord John of Lancaster*, go *you* with him. (Formal.)

2 He is wounded but he will not give in.

3 He is without a scrap of envy and is high in his praise of his brother, the brother who had supplied the place in council he had 'rudely lost', and whom, in their interview together, the King had held up as a model.

Before, I loved thee as a brother, John;
But now, I do respect thee as my soul.

4 He saves the life of his father. (This was the man who had said he was 'like enough . . . to fight against me under Percy's pay'. The King does, however, acknowledge how much mistaken he was in his son.)

5 He kills Hotspur, and pays a generous tribute to a noble foe. So, as he vowed, he has made Hotspur 'render every glory up'. (This is Hotspur's one regret in death, the loss of his 'proud titles', not the loss of 'brittle life'.)

6 Falstaff claims the credit of killing Hotspur, and the Prince says that if it will do him any good he can have it for all he cares. To him the honour was in *doing* the deed, not in the credit he got for it. (Imagine what Hotspur would have said had Falstaff, or any one else, tried to deprive him of the credit for one of *his* victories!)

The Prince's wounds and the King's peril from Douglas have the same effect as Douglas's killing of Blunt (see p.75). Further, the triumph of the Prince over Hotspur is increased. The victor of that combat is a wounded man.

Contrast Hotspur's real death and Falstaff's sham death (when Douglas appears). The Prince sees Falstaff apparently dead, and laconically expresses his feelings when he says 'I could have better spared a better man.' Falstaff later accounts for his counterfeiting death by saying that he was out of breath with fighting Hotspur, whom ultimately he killed!

The scene ends with the trumpet sounding retreat, for the day has been won by the King's army.

make up go into line.
amaze alarm – a much stronger word in Elizabethan English.
stain'd i.e. blood-stained.
point i.e. of his sword.
With lustier maintenance more energetically standing his ground.
Hydra A many-headed snake-like monster, slain by Hercules. See note on 'Hercules', p.50.

very real, true.

win conquer, overcome.

Shirley, Stafford, Blunt Slain by the rebels in the fight. We have seen the killing of Blunt by Douglas in Act V, Sc. iii. Sir Nicholas Gawsey and Clifton are two other leaders on the King's side.

Who never . . . pay True in more ways than one. cf. III. ii. 158–9.

thy lost opinion the reputation you had lost.

tender of regard for, concern for.

hearken'd for waited in hopes of hearing of.

insulting injuring.

your end causing your death.

Make . . . Gawsey He sanctions the strategy decided on by the Prince.

Harry Monmouth See note p.74.

Two . . . sphere Each planet was supposed to be set in a certain sphere.

vanities empty boasts.

titles honours, achievements.

my flesh wounds my flesh.

and life time's fool Therefore thoughts (and the wounds the thinkers have received) even more so are the fool of time and dependent on it. When life goes all must go.

a stop i.e. for every individual – all men bow to death.

Ill-weaved i.e. ill-planned. Hotspur's courage was great, but the ambitions to which he applied it were wrong.

bound See note p.65.

sensible See note on 'insensible', p.73.

favours a handkerchief or scarf, lit. a gift as a mark of favour.

I could . . . man the loss of a better man would have affected me less deeply.

have a heavy miss of thee miss thee greatly.

dearer Punning on 'deer'.

Embowell'd having the bowels removed as a preliminary to having the body embalmed.

powder pickle.

termagant Name of an imaginary Mohammedan god, and applied to a ranting, brawling character in the morality plays, which is what would be in the mind of Shakespeare and at once come to the mind of his audience.

scot and lot with a clean sweep.

if he should counterfeit too and rise The very idea shows the utter impossibility of a man like Falstaff understanding the pursuit of honour which inspired a man like Hotspur.

Nothing . . . eyes only a man looking on could prove me a liar, i.e. by saying that I did not kill Hotspur.

Did you . . . dead? The Prince has had only a short time to be with Lancaster, yet his regard for Falstaff is such that even in this short time he has told him of Falstaff's (apparent) death.

fantasy fancy.

not a double man He would seem this with Hotspur on his back, and, of course, he is at the same time joking about his figure again.

Jack See note p.62.

so See note p.76.

look expect.

a long hour by Shrewsbury clock Such an accomplished liar as Falstaff would naturally trick out his tale with a touch of circumstantial detail like this to add credence to it.

Upon my death We should say 'on my *life*'.

grace favour.

gild i.e. say it is true, echo it. The Prince does exactly the same thing for Falstaff as Vernon does for Worcester (V. ii. 26). We admire the one and despise the other. What makes the difference ? See pp.18–9.)

highest highest part – whence they would get a good view.

Act V Scene v

Victory having rewarded the King's arms, nothing more remains but judgment on the captive rebels. Worcester and Vernon, the two men who have caused a battle which might have been avoided, merit instant death. We admire the King for pausing before judgment on the others. He will judge them calmly, and not be vindictive in the hour of victory. One of them is Douglas, and the Prince begs power to dispose of him. It is at once granted, whereupon he graciously gives his brother the honour of telling Douglas he is a free man : he cherishes, he says, even in an adversary, such valiant deeds as Douglas has wrought.

The play ends with the King outlining his plans to crush the rebels who still remain under arms – those who have not brought their forces to the battle of Shrewsbury. This aim is accomplished in *Henry IV, Part II*. Really *Henry IV, Parts I and II* form *one* play, divided into two to suit the customary length of a theatrical performance.

Thus . . . rebuke The King is rather self-righteous here. His own rebellion against Richard II had not found such rebuke.

Ill-spirited cf. I. i. 97, where Westmoreland's word for Worcester is 'malevolent'.

turn our offers contrary say our offers were the opposite to what they really were.

tenour nature, conditions.

pause defer sentence.

The noble Percy slain See p.11.

Upon the foot of fear fleeing in fear.

prelate Scroop . . . arms See Act IV, Sc. iv.

leave cease.

Revision questions on Act V

1 For what reasons does Worcester bring back a false message to Hotspur?

2 Criticize the way the battle is represented on the stage.

3 Mention any minor successes gained by the rebels before their final defeat and state their dramatic effect.

4 How does Falstaff bring a laugh even to a battle-field?

5 Are you glad that the Prince killed Hotspur?

6 Describe in detail how everything goes to show the glory of the Prince in this Act.

7 Make a few comments on the King's bearing in the hour of victory.

Questions

1 State the grievances of the rebels.

2 What were the reasons for the failure of the rebellion?

3 Make a list in order of the disposition of scenes or parts of scenes as between main and sub-plot. Then indicate the changes from verse to prose or prose to verse, stating what you think is the reason for each change.

4 Which character do you think is the chief connecting link between plot and sub-plot? Indicate in what way.

5 With which party do you sympathise (a) at the beginning of the play, (b) at the end? If your sympathies have changed, account for this.

6 Mention the chief departures from historical fact in *Henry IV, Part I* and state what you take to be the dramatic reasons for them.

7 Give a short account of the dramatic construction of *Henry IV, Part I*.

8 Mention any references in the play to contemporary sports or pastimes.

9 Write a short essay on the character of the King, pointing out what he has in common with Worcester.

10 What ideas of kingship do you find in *Henry IV, Part I*, implied or expressed?

11 'Dissolute; undutiful towards his father; cold-hearted and calculating. His sole redeeming feature is his courage.' Comment on this view of Prince Hal.

12 Did the Prince restrain or encourage his tavern companions in their reckless behaviour?

13 What do we learn of the Prince (a) from what others say of him, (b) from his own actions?

14 Describe the Prince as seen by (a) the King, (b) Hotspur, (c) Falstaff.

15 Contrast the Prince and Hotspur in two parallel columns.

16 'Judge a man's character by what he says of other people, not by what other people say of him.' By this standard, who is the finer, the Prince or Hotspur?

17 How far is Hotspur's reputation justified by his words and actions in the play?

18 Show how Hotspur's character is brought out by his behaviour to (a) his friends, (b) his enemies.

19 (a) For what reasons does Prince Henry enjoy the company of Falstaff? (b) Does Falstaff enjoy the company of the Prince, or does he seek it merely for his own advantage? Support your answer from the play.

20 'We ought not to like this "grey iniquity", but we all do' (p.17). Comment on this observation on Falstaff.

21 'Three masterful men dominate the action of *Henry IV, Part I*, – King Henry, Falstaff and Hotspur.' How far is it true to class all three as 'masterful'?

22 What is the attitude towards honour of (a) the Prince, (b) Hotspur, (c) Falstaff? Prove what you say from their words and actions in the play.

23 How far is (a) Worcester, (b) Hotspur responsible for the rebellion?

24 Discuss the importance in *Henry IV, Part I* of (a) Glendower, (b) Douglas, (c) Lady Percy.

25 History plays inevitably lack female characters. Comment on Shakespeare's success in introducing women into *Henry IV, Part I*.

26 (a) Which character in the play is particularly fitted for planning a conspiracy, and (b) which for leadership?

27 Give what you consider the most outstanding example in the play of (a) loyalty, (b) treachery.

28 Give the substance of any two soliloquies and in each case say what they show of the character of the speaker.

29 How does Shakespeare convey the idea of impetuosity in a speaker?

30 Write an essay on Shakespeare's sense of humour, based on the character of Falstaff.

31 Make a list of as many different kinds of humour as you can find in *Henry IV, Part I*.

32 Choose five examples of Shakespeare's imagery which appeal to you and say why you like them.

33 Which part in the play would you most like to act? Which do you think is the most difficult part to act? In each case give your reasons.

34 What features of *Henry IV, Part I* may be ascribed to Elizabethan stage conditions?

35 Describe an imaginary visit to an Elizabethan theatre for a performance of *Henry IV, Part I*.

Pan study aids Titles published in the Brodie's Notes series

W. H. Auden Selected Poetry

Jane Austen Emma Mansfield Park Northanger Abbey Persuasion
Pride and Prejudice

Anthologies of Poetry Ten Twentieth Century Poets
The Poet's Tale

Samuel Beckett Waiting for Godot

Arnold Bennett The Old Wives' Tale

William Blake Songs of Innocence and Experience

Robert Bolt A Man for All Seasons

Harold Brighouse Hobson's Choice

Charlotte Brontë Jane Eyre

Emily Brontë Wuthering Heights

Robert Browning Selected Poetry

John Bunyan The Pilgrim's Progress

Geoffrey Chaucer (parallel texts) The Franklin's Tale The Knight's
Tale The Miller's Tale The Nun's Priest's Tale The Pardoner's Tale
Prologue to the Canterbury Tales The Wife of Bath's Tale

Richard Church Over the Bridge

John Clare Selected Poetry and Prose

Samuel Coleridge Selected Poetry and Prose

Wilkie Collins The Woman in White

William Congreve The Way of the World

Joseph Conrad The Nigger of the Narcissus & Youth
The Secret Agent

Charles Dickens Bleak House David Copperfield Dombey and Son
Great Expectations Hard Times Little Dorrit Oliver Twist
Our Mutual Friend A Tale of Two Cities

Gerald Durrell My Family and Other Animals

George Eliot Middlemarch The Mill on the Floss Silas Marner

T. S. Eliot Murder in the Cathedral Selected Poems

Henry Fielding Joseph Andrews

F. Scott Fitzgerald The Great Gatsby

E. M. Forster Howard's End A Passage to India
Where Angels Fear to Tread

William Golding Lord of the Flies The Spire

Henry V Julius Caesar King Lear King Richard III
Love's Labour Lost Macbeth Measure for Measure
The Merchant of Venice A Midsummer Night's Dream
Much Ado about Nothing Othello Richard II Romeo and Juliet
The Sonnets The Taming of the Shrew The Tempest
Twelfth Night The Winter's Tale

G. B. Shaw Androcles and the Lion Arms and the Man
Caesar and Cleopatra The Doctor's Dilemma Pygmalion Saint Joan

Richard Sheridan Plays of Sheridan: The Rivals; The Critic;
The School for Scandal

John Steinbeck The Grapes of Wrath Of Mice and Men & The
Pearl

Tom Stoppard Rosencrantz and Guildenstern are Dead

J. M. Synge The Playboy of the Western World

Jonathan Swift Gulliver's Travels

Alfred Tennyson Selected Poetry

William Thackeray Vanity Fair

Flora Thompson Lark Rise to Candleford

Dylan Thomas Under Milk Wood

Anthony Trollope Barchester Towers

Mark Twain Huckleberry Finn

Keith Waterhouse Billy Liar

Evelyn Waugh Decline and Fall Scoop

H. G. Wells The History of Mr Polly

John Webster The White Devil

Oscar Wilde The Importance of Being Earnest

Virginia Woolf To the Lighthouse

William Wordsworth The Prelude (Books 1, 2)

John Wyndham The Chrysalids

W. B. Yeats Selected Poetry

Australian titles

George Johnston My Brother Jack

Thomas Keneally The Chant of Jimmie Blacksmith

Ray Lawler Summer of the Seventeenth Doll

Henry Lawson The Bush Undertaker & Selected Short Stories

Ronald McKie The Mango Tree

Kenneth Slessor Selected Poems

Ralph Stow The Merry-Go-Round in the Sea To the Islands

Patrick White The Tree of Man

David Williamson The Removalists